MEN IN BLACK

Personal Stories & Eerie Adventures

Published by Lisa Hagan Books 2015

Powered by

SHADOW
TEAMS

Copyright © Nick Redfern.

ISBN: 978-0-9764986-6-7

Cover design and interior layout by Simon Hartshorne

— Nick Redfern —

MEN IN BLACK

Personal Stories & Eerie Adventures

Contents

Introduction

I was just eleven years of age when I was introduced to the menacing and macabre world of the enigmatic Men in Black, those dark-suited ghouls that terrorize UFO witnesses and researchers alike.

It was late on a typically – and most appropriately - bleak and windswept English evening when their occult presence first darkened my door. On the night in question – wide of eye and full of youthful, pre-teen excitement and anticipation - I eagerly began reading the disturbing-yet-compelling pages of John Keel's now-classic title, *The Mothman Prophecies*, which told of distinctly strange goings-on at Point Pleasant, West Virginia in the mid-to-late 1960s. Come to think of it, "strange goings-on" may not be the correct terminology to use. Outright paranormal foulness and malignancy would be far more apt, methinks.

A fiery-eyed winged-thing, surreal reports of contact with enigmatic alien intelligences on lonely, moonlit, tree-shrouded roads, occult phenomena plaguing the entire town by the dead of night, and lives manipulated and transformed in ways near-unimaginable, were the order of the day.

And then there was the brooding, predatory, and repeated manifestations of the dreaded MIB that, I got the distinct impression, were pulling the supernatural strings of just about all those myriad entities and unspeakable things that had chosen Point Pleasant as their targets.

For reasons I have never truly been able to fathom, from that very day onwards I became particularly fascinated by the actions of the Men in Black, their silencing of UFO witnesses, their near-ethereal presence in our world, and, of course, their overwhelming and mysterious elusiveness. Who, or more likely what, were they? From where did they originate? What did they want of us? Why were they so deeply intent on silencing Flying Saucer-seekers? Even as a child, and particularly so on those proverbial dark and stormy English nights that seemed all-dominating, such questions plagued and tormented my mind. And, the further and deeper I dug into the subject, the more I found myself attempting to penetrate the veil of unsettling darkness and hostility that seemed to forever surround the MIB.

In the immediate years that followed my reading of John Keel's legendary study of Mothman, I sought out just about as many works on the MIB as was conceivably possible. And, at the absolute top of my list – in undeniably joint first-place - were Gray Barker's 1956 title *They Knew Too Much about Flying Saucers* and a small and overwhelmingly bizarre book titled *Flying Saucers and the Three Men*. The latter was penned in 1962 by a curious and undeniably paranoid character named Albert Bender, without whom there simply would be no MIB puzzle. Period.

Barker, a skilled, atmospheric, Gonzo-style writer with a flair for all-things dramatic, gothic, and turbulent, was the perfect person to address the MIB mystery – even though a self-admitted combination of embellishment, parable and exaggeration was his typical and controversial style. But, Barker would never have been in a position to do much, at all, of a MIB nature had it not been for the eccentric and occult-obsessed Bender, who, in 1953, was allegedly silenced by a trio of black-garbed, blazing-eyed entities from some strange netherworld after getting too close to the truth about Flying Saucers.

Far less Mulder and Scully, and far more H.P. Lovecraft meets *Devil Girl from Mars* meets Bram Stoker, *Flying Saucers and the Three Men* presented the MIB not as government agents of the Will Smith and Tommy Lee Jones variety, but as harshly cold and emotionless aliens who seemed to be unsettlingly familiar with all matters alchemic, occult and nightmarish as they were with UFOs and faraway, fantastic worlds.

Appearing as well-dressed, pale-faced corpses, the terrible trio intimidated and terrified the obsessive-compulsive Bender to the point of near physical and emotional collapse. No wonder he quit UFOlogy and moved onto other things, such as obsessing over the works of Austrian composer, Max Steiner, who was responsible for the soundtracks to the original of *King Kong* and *Gone with the Wind*.

Indeed, in 1965, Bender established the Max Steiner Music Society, and left his old life firmly in the past. As for

Barker, in 1984, it was ill-health, rather than the black-garbed ones, that took him before he reached sixty. Keel continued on for a quarter of a century after Barker, still caught up in - yet never ever quite resolving - the conundrum of the three shadowy men from beyond the veil.

As a kid, I found the books and tales of both Barker and Bender to be even more captivating than those of Keel; despite the fact that out of the three of them, it was Keel who, in the popularity stakes, soared. Of course, as my teens became my twenties, and then my thirties, my views on the MIB phenomenon changed, in some ways subtly, but in other ways far less so. But there was one thing that never did alter: My earnest wish to solve the puzzle of the true nature, origin and intent of the Men in Black. Since those days of my childhood, I have pursued the MIB on a scale that has easily far exceeded my quests for the truth about Bigfoot, the Chupacabras, and Roswell combined.

My first book, *A Covert Agenda*, which was published in 1997, detailed a number of curious MIB-style encounters in the British Isles from the 1950s onwards. My 2003 title, *Strange Secrets*, included a chapter on the little-known issue of government files on the Men in Black. Three years later, I penned *On the Trail of the Saucer Spies*, which was a full-length study of the secret surveillance of certain elements of the UFO research community by MIB-type characters in government.

Then, in 2011, *The Real Men in Black* hit the bookshelves.

This latter title from me specifically addressed the paranormal side of the MIB phenomenon. And, in that same year, I was very pleased to be asked to write a new foreword to an updated and expanded edition of Gray Barker's 1983 book: *M.I.B.: The Secret Terror among Us*, as well as a paper for Timothy Green Beckley's mighty tome, *Curse of the Men in Black*.

In other words, while I have never been fortunate enough to have received a late-night visit from the terrible MIB (Yes, I *would* consider such a visit to be fortunate, as I might then be able to finally answer the riddle of who or what *they* really are), they have certainly got their grips into me in other ways. Having written about, and pondered so extensively on, the Men in Black, would I consider my research in this area to be a full-blown obsession? No. I prefer the word fascination. I should stress that pursuing the MIB is not something that – in any way, at all - impacts upon my social life or my day-to-day activities, but, even so, they never really go away. They're always lurking, hovering in the shadows, and forever just out of reach.

I'm certainly not the first – nor will I be the last – to be pulled, magnet-like, into the turbulent eye of the MIB hurricane. Bender, Barker, Keel: they all came before me, and all three became truly enveloped by MIB high-strangeness. And, doubtless, there will be those Men in Black seekers who will follow me down the rabbit-hole in which the MIB dwell darkly while carefully plotting their nefarious actions. But, in the meantime, my work in this particular arena is far from done – which is precisely why you are now devouring these very pages.

As is often the case when someone writes a book, those who read it and who have a story, or sometimes several, to tell will contact the author and relate the facts. As far as the MIB are concerned, that has now happened to me on countless occasions. But, purely for space reasons and to ensure that my editors do not find themselves suffering from near MIB-overload, many of the accounts I have on-file of personal and extraordinary encounters with the Men in Black have never seen the light of day.

At least, they haven't until now.

It's fair to say that my latest book on the Men in Black is somewhat of a radical departure for me, in the sense that I have specifically let the witnesses and the theorists – certainly, the most important people when it comes to trying to understand the nature of the MIB phenomenon – tell their own stories, solely in their own words. My role, here, is merely to introduce you to the plethora of players in the seemingly never-ending saga of the crazed and creepy Men in Black, and have them relate their amazing and intriguing stories.

It was my original intention to write a kind of "summary-analysis"-type section after each respective report or paper. But, then, after having given the matter deep thought, I decided otherwise. At the end of the day, we all have our views and opinions on the nature and actions of the MIB, and giving my opinion on each and every bit of data would be as pointless as it would be tedious and undeniably repetitive. Instead, I leave it up to the witnesses and the investigators to share their data, and I leave it up to you to digest that same data as you see fit.

In some cases, the information is scant, but tantalizing. In others, it is lengthy and twisting. In a few, it's downright controversial to just about the ultimate degree of impossible. But, in all cases, the data is – just like the MIB themselves – uncanny, unsettling, and deeply bizarre. So, with the above all said, I now invite you to sit back – on what I most earnestly hope will be for you what it was for me the first time I encountered the MIB, namely a dark, shadowy and chilled eve – and immerse yourself in countless sinister tales of the Men in Black...

1.

"Men in Black types
have pounced on humanity"

Rich Reynolds is a long-time commentator on, and observer of, the UFO phenomenon. He is a prestigious blogger and someone who is not afraid to offer his views on the UFO subject and its many and varied attendant controversies. A man with a profound knowledge of the flying saucer phenomenon, and someone possessed of a keen eye and an even keener bullshit-detector, Rich can be found online at http://ufocon. blogspot.com

The Men in Black, whom Nick Redfern has documented rather fully in his book, *The Real Men in Black*, have been with mankind for a lot longer than surmised. They ensued right after the dawn of civilization, if The Hebrew Bible (the Old Testament) and various myths have any reportorial accuracy. The modern-day MIB phenomenon began with Gray Barker's introduction of them in his 1956 book, *They Knew Too Much About Flying Saucers*. However, those versed in early religious and mythological tales know that Men in Black types have pounced on humanity well before 1956. The difference, which seems to have thrown off MIB enthusiasts, is that those early "men" were garbed in white; Men in White, as it were.

The Bible is replete with such encounters: Genesis 18/19: Verses 1 through 29 (in Chapter 19) recounts the visitation of God and/or his angels, telling Abraham about a pending birth and the destruction of Sodom and Gomorrah. Chapter 22 of Genesis tells of a visitation by a "man in white" who instructs Abraham to take his son Isaac up into the mountains to kill him. (This "man in white" was a psychopathic jokester it turns out.) Genesis Chapter 28: Verse 10 tells how Jacob, in a transcendental dream state was visited by the ultimate Man in White (God) and a legion of men in white (angels) who ascended and descended a ladder, as the Man in White offered to give Jacob the land upon which he was resting.

3 Kings 19: Verses 9 though19 provides the story of Elias being visited by the Man in White who tells him that those who worshipped the false god, Baal, will be destroyed and Elias will anoint Jehu the king of Israel. Chapter 11 of Tobias has a man in white giving Tobias the power to return sight to his (Tobias') father.

And the famous Ezekiel passages, so enamored by UFO buffs, opens with a visitation by a man with the appearance of fire who told Ezekiel of abominations in Judah and that he was sending men in white to avenge his (the man of fire's) wrath. Chapter 9 opens with six men appearing at the gate to the city; one man, clothed in linen, had an inkhorn in his hand with which to mark those who had transgressed the man of fire's proscriptions. The mark, Thau, was to be placed on all who had sinned: men, old and young, women, old and young, pity offered to no sinner.

Chapter 10 continues the story with the man clothed in linen carrying out the man of fire's dicta culminating in the chariot of fire (the UFO imagined by Blumrich et al.). Daniel 9:20 introduces Gabriel, a ubiquitous man in white, to Daniel. Gabriel offers prophecy and visions. Then in Daniel 13 (appendix), verses 28 ff. some "men in black" do appear but Daniel proclaimed those men had borne false witness and the people stoned them to death.

In Bullfinch's <u>Age of Fable and Beauties of Mythology</u> [David Mckay, 1898], Chapter VI presents, in the story of Baucis and Philemon, a visitation by Jupiter, in human shape and his son Mercury (without wings) to Phrygia – appearing as travelers – who were treated well by a poor couple (Baucis and Philemon) while the rest of Phrygia's residents didn't. The Gods (men in white) destroyed the village, and made the couple guardians of their temple….

In Chapter IX, Morpheus, at the direction of goddess Juno, assumes the visage of a dead man, Ceyx, to assuage the agony of remorse that his wife, Halcyone, was feeling. Chapter XXII allows a profane person and despiser of the Gods, Erisichthon, to be eviscerated by the Dryades (men/women in white) in the form of Ceres. (Erisichthon had axed a sacred oak tree beloved by Ceres.)

The Bullfinch book (501 pages) is a compendium of

myths from all cultures: Egypt, India, the lands of Norsemen, et cetera. Among the tales told are many where men in white appear, to rectify wrongs (or cause trouble sometimes).

Two obscure accounts about visitations by Men in White (or Black) can be found in the story of Socrates who was approached by a " divine being" when he served in the Greek army and the amorphous being who greeted Malcolm X in his jail cell.

That human beings have been visited by Men in Black (or White) for millennia is a literary truism. Are those visitations real? Tangible? No one has an answer to that. Evidence is oral, not palpable. Have Men in Black harassed UFO witnesses? Nick Redfern thinks so. But, like those religious and mythological tales, there is no real proof that Men in Black or White have actually touched or spoken to anyone.

The hallucinatory aspect of such accounts is not to be dismissed easily; nor are the plethora of such recountings. After all, not everyone who has experienced a visitation by MIB or MIW is crazy…right?

2.

"Looking up at his room, were the three men"

The author/co-author of 181 books, Brad Steiger wrote the paperback bestseller about UFOs *Strangers from the Skies* in 1966. His edited work *Project Bluebook* was hailed by *Omni* magazine as one of the best UFO books of the century. In 1987, Steiger was inducted into the Hypnosis Hall of Fame for his work with UFO contactees, abductees, and past life regression. In Minneapolis, he received the Lifetime Achievement Award at the National UFO and Unexplained Phenomena Conference in 1996.

For many decades, together with his wife Sherry, herself the author/co-author of 45 books and the publicist for Dr. J. Allen Hynek's UFO research group in Phoenix, Brad researched and investigated UFOs and their cultural impact throughout world history. The Steigers have lectured and conducted seminars on the phenomenon throughout the United States and overseas.

The Steigers were featured in 22 episodes of the television series *Could It Be a Miracle?* Together, their television appearances and specials include: *The Joan Rivers Show,*

Entertainment Tonight, Inside Edition, Hard Copy, Hollywood Insider, and specials on HBO, USA Network, The Learning Channel, The History Channel, and Arts and Entertainment (A&E), among others. Their current book is *Real Encounters, Different Dimensions, and Otherworldly Beings.*

Brad Steiger is also someone who knows far more than a bit about the Men in Black, as you will now see…

Who are the Men in Black? – By Brad Steiger

After more than 50 years of research in the UFO and paranormal fields, I have come to the conclusion that many of the mysteries that bedevil us are products of a reflexive phenomenon. This reflexive action does not usually occur in the more mundane pursuits of architecture, industry, mining, agriculture and the like, but once one begins actively to pursue UFOlogy or psychical research, one runs the risk of entering a surreal world in which the usual physical laws do not apply.

In the case of the mythos of the Men in Black, I suggest that that eerie enigma may have begun with the machinations of a human agency assigned to investigate the actions of the more high profile investigators of the phenomenon and the more convincing witness of UFO activity with the goals of learning more about the growing interest in a worldwide phenomena. Somehow along the way, this activity of the human surveillance of other humans caught the interest of a nonhuman, paraphysical agency that has for centuries pursued goals that remain elusive, even sinister, to the individuals whom they visit. Whether motivated by a bizarre sense of humor, an essentially malicious nature, or a desire to learn how much some humans know about their eternal secrets, the Others began knocking on the doors of those who had witnessed or who had investigated UFO activity. Some of my experiences with the MIB seem most certainly the product of human surveillance that in most instances was conducted with awkward fallibility.

Once in the golden era of MIB activity in the late 1960s while speaking to a fellow researcher on the telephone, our conversation was interrupted by a metallic-sounding voice chanting: "Ho, ho, UFO!" Because it seemed that this got a rise out of us, this merry chant was repeated on a number of telephone calls with other investigators.

A friend who had been doing a great deal of research on my behalf told of the time when he was anticipating a visit from me. He picked up the telephone to make a call on his private line, only to hear the following bit of conversation:

"Has Steiger arrived in town yet?"

"Not yet."

"What motel will he be staying in?"

"The [correct name of the motel in which I had made reservations]."

"Don't worry. Everything is set."

At this point my friend broke in and asked who the hell was on his private line. There was a stunned silence, a click, then the steady buzzing of a clear line.

I had my own experience with the awkward telephone spies when I checked into a hotel and found that the bell man had missed one of my suitcases - the most important one with the slides for my lecture.

I picked up the receiver to hear a man's voice inquire: "When is he supposed to check in?"

"He is already in his room," I said in reply, though I knew the query wasn't asked of me.

"Oh, s—t!" was the profound response, followed by two rapid hang-ups.

Other experiences with the MIB are not so easy to place in either the Human or Non-Human category.

A friend of mine was traveling in England before starting on an around-the-world junket with a layover in Vietnam to visit his son in the armed forces. He was walking near a railway station in London when he noticed three men dressed completely in black staring at him.

When my friend returned their collective stare, they approached him and asked him which train they should take for such-and-such a city. My friend calmly pointed out that he was a tourist, and it made a good deal more sense for them to ask at the information booth just a few feet away.

My friend turned on his heel and walked away from the odd trio, but a glance over his shoulder told him that they were still standing there staring at him, unmindful of checking with the information booth. Suddenly ill at ease, my friend hailed a taxi and went directly to his hotel.

When he got to his room, an uncomfortable sensation prickled the back of his neck and he glanced out his window. On the street corner, looking up at his room, were the three men. Baffled, he tried to push the incident from his mind.

A day or so later, though, he was confronted by one of the men who told him straight out: "You are a friend of Brad Steiger. Tell him we shall visit him by Christmas."

My friend had only a peripheral knowledge of the UFO can of worms, but he returned to his hotel room and wrote me a long letter with the above details.

Not long after I had received his letter, I visited a friend in another city and told him about the bizarre experience my correspondent had encountered in London.

"Humph!" Jim snorted over the lunch we were sharing. "If those monkeys come to see you this Christmas, send 'em down to talk to me. I'd love to get one of those characters in my hands. I would solve this man-in-black mystery you've been telling me about!"

I laughed and warned him that he had better be careful or he might get his wish.

I had not returned from my trip by more than a few minutes when the telephone rang. It was Jim calling. Wondering if I might have left something at his place of business, I was informed that I had indeed left a most peculiar something behind me.

Jim told me that I had no sooner started my homeward journey than he was told that a gentleman wished to see him.

A secretary ushered a man of average height into Jim's office. But my friend said that his visitor was the thinnest human being he had ever seen.

"He was cadaverous, Brad," Jim told me. "He looked like those World War II photographs of someone in a concentration camp. But he seemed alert enough, and so involved in his quest that he ignored my proffered hand of greeting. In fact, I tried to push shaking his hand, but he refused to touch me.

"I hear you want to be the head of UFO's in Iowa," he said quickly.

"He took out a wallet, flipped it open, then shut, before I could see any identification. I can't really recall anything else he said, because it was all so damned nonsensical. Soon he was gone, and I was still sitting there dumbfounded.

"I jumped to my feet, though, when I heard his car starting. I got a good look at his automobile and I wrote down its license number. I can't tell you what make of car it was. It looked like a combination of three or four different makes and models, but it didn't really look like anything I had ever seen before. And the license number didn't check. The Highway Patrol said there was no such Iowa plate registered. A friend in another branch of state government, who owed me a favor, said the plate wasn't registered to any government agency, either."

The cases above are baffling, but in the following instances I suspect a human agency involved in a strange campaign that was conducted regarding Steiger imposters who spoke at various conferences around the United States. On occasions the imposters allegedly conducted themselves very well, thus making the whole enterprise of Counterfeit Steigers a seemingly futile project. On other occasions, the imposter's assignment was quite obviously to taint my reputation.

On an unfortunate number of occasions, I received letters complaining of my outrageous and insulting behavior while speaking at a conference. There were claims that I had openly berated my audience, calling them stupid for accepting the very premise of UFOs. A close friend happened to arrive on the scene after one pseudo-Steiger had departed and tried his best to assure the sponsors of the event that the rowdy, disrespectful speaker could not have been the real Brad. In his letter, my friend warned me that he had visited a number of lecture halls where the imposter had damned his audiences.

"Someone seems out to damage your reputation," he advised.

In a most bizarre twist, dozens of men and women have approached me at various lectures and seminars, congratulating me about the manner in which I bested Dr. Carl Sagan in debate. The event allegedly occurred after a lecture when I happened to bump into the great scientist in a restaurant. The eatery, according to the witnesses, was crowded with those who had attended the seminar, and they egged on a debate between myself and Dr. Sagan. I mopped up the floor with him, countering his every argument against the reality of UFOs.

The truth is that I never met Dr. Sagan, therefore, neither

had I ever debated him. But from coast to coast, there are those who claim to have witnessed my triumphal bout.

Even more individuals claim to have been in the audience when I delivered a rousing message from the Space Brothers in Seattle. Regardless of how often I deny that I was not in Seattle at that time and have never channeled the Space Brothers, those who were at that event are puzzled why I would deny my eloquence.

It is true. I have met and interviewed men and women who do claim to speak on behalf of Extraterrestrial Intelligences, but in retrospect, I found such a privilege to carry with it many possible negative experiences. I think of the reminiscences that I have shared of an Iowa farm family from those weird and wild MIB days. UFOs had become a part of this family's life several years before one of its male members became a "channel" for an entity who claimed to be from another world. The invisible telepathic being began communicating with the family because they had been "selected before they had been born" to assist him in doing "His" work and in protecting Earth from another group of intelligences who sought to enslave mankind.

The communicating entity led the various members of the family circle on a number of "assignments" designed to save the Earth and to serve the benign entity and his kind. But always, the entity warned them, there was the enemy group with its men in black, seeking whom they might devour.

The family, who became "flying saucer missionaries,"

saw mysterious fellow passengers board airplanes with them – then disappear somewhere in mid-flight. Automobiles appeared out of nowhere to follow and harass them.

A man claiming to be from a state educational division called at the high school and talked for over an hour with one of the teenaged girl members of the family. The only questions he asked had to do with whether or not she would be able to recognize a spy. When suspicious adult members of the beleaguered family checked with school administrators, they were informed that they had no knowledge of such a man or of such a division within the state educational system. [Interestingly, I have now met a number of adults who claimed such an experience with an MIB. It claimed to be a representative from the state educational division who took them out of class for a "test."]

The girl who had been interrogated by the unidentified man also developed into a "channel" for the communicating entity, and soon several members of the family were practicing automatic writing.

UFO's swooped low overhead at night. Eerie lights were seen to dance about in the fields. Invisible entities snatched keys from their resting places and jangled them about the room, terrifying the children. Unseen hands lifted a mattress on which one couple lay sleeping. Underneath were "secret" papers that the principal communicating entity had dictated.

Their farm work was being ignored. Their lives had become a living nightmare in which every stranger was suspect, every sound in the night that of an invader, every strange coincidence imbued with desperate and weighty significance.

At last the full realization that they had been deceived--that they had been led into a silly game--jolted them into determined action, and they resumed meaningful living, becoming a quite prosperous farm family. Although some of their past experiences seemed foolish in retrospect, they had to agree that they had learned valuable lessons from their strange companions.

Nowadays whenever I review those days of encounters with the men in black, I am led to think of the mythological figure common to all cultures and known generically to ethnologists as the Trickster. The Trickster plays pranks upon mankind, but often at the same time he is instructing them or transforming aspects of the world for the benefit of his human charges.

Most cultures view the Trickster as a primordial being who came into existence soon after the creation of the world. A number of Amerindian tribes referred to their Trickster figure as "Old Man," because they saw him as someone who was ageless, as old as time.

The Trickster is usually viewed as a supernatural being with the ability to change his shape at will. Although basically wily, he may behave in a very stupid, childish manner at times, and may often end up as the one who is tricked. The Trickster lies, cheats, and steals without compunction. He seems often to be the very essence of amoral animalism.

The Trickster figure is often credited with bringing death and pain into the world; yet, in some recitations, his own son was the first to die as a result. Perhaps one day we will learn the positive aspect of the MIB, the Trickster, the UFOnaut. As strange as it may seem, the MIB may merely be attempting to teach in their own strange ways the knowledge, or awareness, of powers that today exist only in our dreams of the future.

3.

"Some witnesses report that the skin looks 'artificial'"

David Weatherly is the author of several books including *Strange Intruders and The Black Eyed Children.* He can be reached at http://www.leprechaunpress.com/ David has deeply studied the parallels between the MIB and the Black-Eyed Children, as he reveals to us in a downright creepy exposé…

Children of the Men in Black – By David Weatherly

The Dreadful Knock

Imagine, it's dusk and you've just begun to settle in for the evening. Your solitude is interrupted when there's a knock at your door. It's a long, continuous rapping, almost maddening in its insistence. Answering the door, you find a young child of about ten years old. He stands quietly in a hooded top and jeans, staring at his shoes. What you see of his face is very pale and for some reason you can't put your finger on, he makes you nervous. In a cold, monotone voice, he requests that you "invite him in."

You look around, wondering where his parents are. You ask if he's lost, or needs help, to which he responds: "Just let me in, this won't take long."

You start to back away but for some reason. You're conflicted. You feel stuck between running and simply opening the door and asking him to step inside. It is, after all, only a child isn't it? That's when he looks up and makes eye contact with you, revealing large solid black eyes that are unlike anything humanly possible. Your unease gives way to outright fear.

Your flight response kicks in and you dash inside, slamming the door and bolting it as quickly as possible. You're shaking from fear and you say a silent prayer that the "boy" will just go away.

You've just encountered a black-eyed kid, now commonly known as a 'BEK.'

What exactly are these strange beings? And what is their bizarre connection to the infamous Men in Black?

Early Encounters

The modern wave of BEK encounters began in the 1990s when Texas journalist Brian Bethel ran into a pair of the kids one evening. He posted his personal account on the Internet and the response was overwhelming to say the least.

Bethel had driven to a local shopping center one evening to drop off a payment at an after-hours mail drop. While sitting in his car writing a check, he was approached by a pair of boys who tried to coax him into offering them a ride. Their mannerisms were strange and Bethel felt that something was amiss as they recounted their story. In fact, he was so nervous that he only rolled his window down slightly, just enough to hear the boys clearly. The two boys claimed to be interested in seeing a movie but had "left their money at home" and needed Bethel to give them a ride to retrieve it. Bethel was sharp enough to notice that the last showing of the movie was more than half over. Something, he knew, was amiss.

Brian continued to feel nervous as he spoke to the kids. Since he was clearly not responsive to the boys, they pressed him further.

"C'mon mister, now, we just want to go to our house, and we're just two little boys."

It was another odd statement and at this point, Bethel made eye contact with the boys. He was shocked to see that they both had solid black eyes.

"They were coal black, no-pupil, no-iris just-two-staring-orbs reflecting the red and white light of the marquee," Bethel recalls.

It was the final straw. Bethel's nervous tension gave way to his flight response and he raced out of the parking lot, leaving the boys behind. He stole a quick look back as he was pulling away and saw that the two disturbing kids were nowhere to be seen.

Brian Bethel was left with a deep sense of fear and dread. He was also quite confused. Although they appeared to be normal boys, the encounter with the pair had made him experience a range of odd feelings and he couldn't shake the experience. He posted the account on the Internet and was surprised at the response. The story struck a chord with readers and people began to list their own encounters with weird black eye beings. Was this the birth of a new urban legend or just the latest manifestation of something much, much older?

Exploring the Connections

Although I had read the early stories, it wasn't until I met a gentleman who had experienced the black-eyed children himself that I turned a serious eye towards investigating the phenomena. As I interviewed more witnesses and dug deeper, I was struck by the fact that the BEKs shared traits with many different types of paranormal phenomena. Arguments could be made that they were alien hybrids, demons, ghosts or a host of other beings. One of the most intriguing connections that arose, however, were the similarities between the BEKs and the strange Men in Black or, MIB.

On the surface, there may seem to be few connections between the UFO connected MIB and creepy little kids with black eyes showing up on doorsteps. But, when we delve into the actual accounts, we find numerous similarities.

Consider the appearance of both beings. The BEKs are usually described as having pale or pasty skin. Some witnesses report that the skin looks "artificial." Still other accounts claim that the children have olive toned skin that implies they are of Mediterranean origin. Both of these descriptions are heard in classic MIB encounters. Oddly, no one who has ever encountered the BEKs report a blemish of any kind. Bear in mind, these are children usually in their pre-teen years. One would expect acne, pimples, freckles, something, but it's never the case.

Next is the manner of speech. The black-eyed children are reported to speak in a very monotone manner. Their use of language is often awkward and unusual. They will use phrases that simply aren't natural such as "Is it food time?" Perhaps even more troubling, many people who encounter the BEKs believe that the children are attempting to exert some type of mind control through the use of repeated phrases and their cold, monotone speech patterns. Typical MIB encounters certainly contain elements of attempted coercion by the strange gentlemen as witnesses to UFO sightings are encouraged to ignore what they saw. Are the attempts by the children another form of this same control dynamic?

Not only are the BEKs awkward in their communication efforts, they also appear unfamiliar with common objects that most of us use on a daily basis.

Take the case of Susan, for instance. She encountered the BEKs at her home in the Orlando, Florida area. Susan was hard at work finishing a project when the knocking started.

"I'll be honest", she says. "I was in a very bad mood. The day had been very frustrating and I hadn't really gotten much done. I was focused on my project when the knocking started. I was trying to finish something, just one little piece, and thought that the person at the door would just wait for a moment. The knocking didn't stop though, not even a break, it was long and constant. I got very angry about it for some reason. I dropped what I was doing and went to the door"

Susan reports that she flung the door open very quickly because of her anger. She barely noticed the two kids standing on her porch as she took a step out and pointed at her doorbell button.

"Why don't you use the damn doorbell?" She shouted. The response she received was very odd to say the least. The two children turned their heads and looked at the lit doorbell button, then slowly turned and looked back at Susan.

"They repeated this motion several times. It was as if they had no idea what that button was for or what I meant by my question. I honestly don't think they knew what a doorbell was.

"I suddenly felt very uncomfortable. It was a creepy response and I took a step back so that I was in my doorway."

After an uncomfortable pause, one of the kids turned back to Susan and requested that she ask them in.

"He kept saying that I should invite them in because it was hot outside. I'd never seen these kids before in my life and I certainly wasn't going to let them in my house. What's weird is that at the time, it almost made sense to me and I actually thought about opening the door and letting them come inside. I just felt completely confused. I kept thinking about the doorbell though and why they acted like they didn't know what it was. The kid who was speaking finally looked up and stared directly at me. That's when I saw the eyes, solid black. Frankly it scared me like nothing ever had. I ran inside and slammed the door, locking the deadbolt."

The weird reaction of the children to the doorbell harkens back to MIB encounters where the Men in Black exhibit confusion when presented with forks or cups of jello. If these were normal humans, why would they have such trouble with common objects? Adding to the strangeness, no one has ever reported a BEK with an iPod or cell phone. That in itself is most unusual for the modern age. How many children could one spot on a daily basis that aren't texting or plugged in to music? With the common use of small hand-held devices, the answer is very few.

Evan in Illinois encountered a BEK who wanted a ride to some vague location. He handed the boy his cell phone and told him that he could call his parents if he needed a ride. The puzzled boy turned the phone over and over in his hands as if he'd never seen such a device and had no idea what to do with it.

Evan addressed the boy; "Don't you know your Mom's number?"

After a pause, the boy replied; "Six."

The boy looked up when he answered revealing solid black eyes. Stunned, Evan quickly drove away leaving the boy and the cell phone behind. He reported the phone stolen but it never turned up.

BEKs in the Machine

While the black eye kid in Evan's encounter seemed unable to do anything with a cell phone, it hasn't stopped his cohorts from causing trouble with electronic devices on other occasions. Indeed, like the MIB, the BEKs have entered the realm of electronic interference.

While I received a few minor reports of such things when doing research, it was only after the publication of my book, *The Black Eyed Children*, that things got really interesting.

The first indications came in the aftermath of the book's release. Appearing on various radio shows and podcasts to discuss the topic, some odd things began to occur. I found that I could talk about a wide range of paranormal topics, but, when the discussion turned to the black eyed children, things changed. Electronic issues would suddenly plague the program. Strange sounds and static would interrupt the show. Calls would be dropped and weird clicking noises would come from nowhere.

Appearing on *Dreamland* with Whitley Strieber, technical issues started right from the beginning. Twice we were disconnected after strange sounds on the line. This could be easily dismissed but the problems didn't end there. The volume levels of the show were all over the place as Whitley recorded.

"I've never seen this happen before" Whitley reported as he attempted to correct the issues in his studio. I'll note here that Whitley and I discussed both the MIB and the BEK.

In fact, on this particular show, Whitley revealed for the first time that he himself had encountered a black-eyed child.

But weird electronic events were not restricted to interviews. Strange as it sounds, I began to receive some accounts of people experiencing such events while they were researching the BEKs themselves.

The first email came from a reader name Jane. She writes in part:

"Every time I start reading your book, *The Black Eyed Children*, electronics in my house go wonky. The first night the smoke alarm went off even though there was no smoke. The second evening the timer on my stove went crazy. I never set it and never use it so that was weird; I didn't even know what it was at first. Then another time my garage door opened itself! That one really freaked me out! Are other people having such weird things happen or is this some strange coincidence? I'm interested in the topic but I honestly don't want any black eyed kids showing up at my door!"

Indeed, Jane was not alone in her experience. About a dozen readers reported similar incidents and sent me questions or comments similar to the above. It's a small number by comparison, but still notable.

Psychic Kimberly Rackley had a similar experience:

"Since I ordered your book I have been having issues with computer, Internet and modem. Last night while listening to GDC...the show suddenly stopped. No tech difficulties could be found to solve...they are blaming the server, the host was baffled at the problem and guess what? Your book was sitting right next to my computer of which I read most of the day and had notes of my impressions laying on top of the book."

Jane and Kimberly certainly were not alone and the incidents were not always instigated by simply reading the book. Other people reported their attempts to research the black eyed children on the Internet and having strange results.

Shannon in Illinois reports:

"For some reason, out of the blue, I suddenly found myself compelled by stories of black eyed kids. A friend told me an encounter that was supposed to have happened on a Marine base in North Carolina. Even after a few days, I couldn't get the story out of my mind so I decided to do some research. My husband and son had gone to bed, it was about ten o'clock and I wasn't tired. I started looking up information on the Internet about the BEKs.

Just as I was reading the Brian Bethel story, all the power went out. It came back on after a few minutes and I restarted my computer. I looked outside and wondered what had happened since the skies were clear. I went right back to my research and again, right in the middle of reading through a website about the BEKs, the power went off. I went through the whole cycle again. The third time when I had started the computer and got to reading, the power flickered and the light bulb in my desk lamp exploded. It scared me so much; I jumped up and went to get in bed with my husband. The next day, I was home alone and decided to try again. Appliances in my house started to malfunction. The microwave started beeping and nothing was in it. I finally had to unplug it. When I did, I still heard a beeping noise and realized that my alarm clock was going off too so I also had to unplug it to get it to stop. Once again, the computer went down as soon as I was on a website reading black eyed kid information. This time though, I was on my husband's computer so I knew it wasn't an issue with my computer. Since then, every time I start to research the black eyed kids, strange things like this happen. Part of me wants to leave it alone, but honestly, I can't seem to help myself. I've decided though that I'll do the rest of my research at the local library. I guess I feel like maybe there's safety in numbers."

Over time, several of those who experienced electronic issues while researching the BEKs began to recover memories of their own encounters with the odd children.

"It all seems rather surreal" Jane later told me. "I did some therapy to recover my repressed memories and there were those kids, buried in my past. I guess somehow, reading about them triggered a release of the memory and it turns out that I had my own encounter with them. I'm happy that I'm still around but I think I'll leave the subject alone, I couldn't bear for those things to return."

Had Jane herself caused the electrical malfunctions in her home or was some other, outside force involved? Are the MIB and the BEKs related in some way? The more we delve into the effects on electronic items, the more possible such connections appear. Perhaps the BEKs and the MIB simply operate on the same frequency. Hence, the effects on witnesses is similar.

Point Pleasant Calling

On a personal level, these weird, electronic related events reached a crescendo in the spring of 2012. It started, simply enough, with a phone call.

Sitting in my office one afternoon, my cell phone lit up. Since the number was programmed in, I knew who was calling. It was a friend and fellow investigator of the paranormal, Jeff Waldridge. Answering the phone however, I was not greeted with Jeff's voice, merely static. No problem, I thought, he had probably pocket dialed my number.

Had it happened once or even a couple of times, I would have dismissed it but this became a constant occurrence over the next several days. I knew it wasn't an issue with the phone since all other calls I received were static free. Since I was extremely busy at the time, I didn't address the frequent calls right away, expecting them to stop. They didn't. The phone would ring when I was nowhere around, resulting in long messages left on my voice mail filled with static and garbled sounds.

Listening to one of the messages one morning, I heard the sound of a child's voice. Here was the answer I thought, Jeff's child had been playing with his phone and hitting the call button on my number. I sent a text letting him know that his child had been playing with his phone and calling me repeatedly. He was a bit puzzled, but checked his call log, saw the calls and apologized with a promise that it wouldn't happen again. Of course, it did. In fact, the calls seemed to increase and come at even more random hours. The phone would ring in the middle of the night, or, sometimes, it would ring when I stepped away from my desk for just a moment, leaving nothing but a missed log and another message of static. I emailed Jeff, but he simply couldn't explain what was happening.

One particular night, just after one of these calls, I received an email from Jeff. He recounted to me that he was lying on his bed, reading *The Black Eyed Children*. Suddenly, his phone lit up.

"…I was reading *The Black Eyed Children* book. The phone was laying about six inches from me and it started dialing you. It was the craziest thing I've seen."

Jeff was puzzled by the phone not just activating itself, but dialing my number without anyone touching it. Following up on all possibilities, he took the cell phone to his provider and explained the mystery. They too were mystified that the phone appeared to act on its own accord and that it only dialed one number - mine. Phone technicians could not explain the situation. Nothing in the phone was broken so no repairs were done. The calls continued. Whoever or whatever was playing games still had a point to make.

Like me, Jeff has a wide range of interest in the paranormal, UFOs, cryptids and conspiracy theories. He investigates sites on a regular basis and takes trips when he gets the time. Neither of us was sure exactly what the calls meant and there was certainly no pattern that either of us could detect.

The finale was about to come and it was quite a statement. Jeff went on a road trip. Naturally he carried his cell phone with him. It was during this trip that the last call came in. His phone was sitting on the dash of the car and lit up dialing my number when Jeff drove into Point Pleasant, WV.

No doubt, most readers will recognize the town as the home of that flying, red-eyed entity known as the Mothman. Point Pleasant had its share of MIB sightings during the height of the Mothman's activity. Legendary investigator of the strange, John Keel, was actually threatened by a trio of MIB who told him to leave both the Mothman and UFOs alone.

Whatever was manipulating the cell phone could not have picked a better place from which to make a final statement. Such high strangeness only added to the mystery. Questions remained. Who, or what, was causing the calls and frequent electronic interference? Was it the MIB, the BEKs, or both? Not only that, but what exactly was the point they were trying to make? The rabbit hole, it seemed, became deeper all the time.

It is interesting to note that, while many people considered the Mothman to be an omen of impending disaster, the BEKs are at times cast in the same light. Numerous people who have encountered the creepy children believe they were an omen of ill fortune. Some report that after seeing the kids, they experienced misfortunes, losses and at times, even deaths in their family. Like the Mothman, there is debate as to whether the black eyed children bring disaster or simply appear in advance of impending ill fortune.

A Strange Alphabet Soup

BEKs, MIB and of course UFOs, do they all fit together somehow? I'm frequently asked if encounters with the BEKs have any correlation to UFO sightings. One would almost expect this given the strange nature of the encounters, the weird similarities between the Men in Black and the black eyed children and the general strangeness surrounding UFOs. Oddly, so far, there are few connections between accounts of UFO sightings and appearances of the BEKs. In fact, it seems as though the BEK may actually avoid locations during times of high UFO activity.

It's almost contrary to MIB accounts when the gentlemen show up directly after UFO sightings to harass the witnesses. Given the high number of UFO reports in recent years, one would expect that a certain percent of black eyed child encounters would occur at the same time but it doesn't seem to be the case. Furthermore, a portion of those people who report BEK encounters (around 10-15 percent) are also abductees. Many of these people report frequent sightings of UFOs, yet their BEK encounters happen on separate occasions.

John Keel's encounter with the MIB in his home was shared with Nick Redfern by author Brad Steiger.

Steiger reported that Keel "…began to tell me of the visitations he'd had with three men who had not knocked, but had entered, his apartment. They literally came *through* the door." Others who have encountered the MIB have reported the same sudden invasion of their homes by the weird figures. The MIB, it seems, do not need to be invited inside. Oddly, this is the opposite of typical BEK encounters. When the black eyed children show up, they spend most of their time trying to convince their victim to "invite them in."

Still, there remain odd connections between the MIB and the BEKs. Encounters with both beings are tense and nerve wracking. Many who have encountered the black eyed children believe they have experienced something very sinister.

"I felt like I was being eyed up and down by a predator" reports John.

"I served in the military and I was in combat. I know what it feels like to have something that wants to harm you staring at you. It's a bad feeling in the gut and the hair on the back of your neck stands up. That's what I felt that night and it's a damned odd thing that I'll never understand. They looked like kids except for those black eyes."

John echoes the feelings that many other witnesses express. Regardless of the childlike appearance, it's clear that the BEKs are far from normal children. Are they connected to the notorious MIB? Perhaps they are the latest version of some otherworldly or other dimensional creatures that use our reality as a playground or worse, a laboratory.

"I'm convinced they're connected to UFOs somehow" John states. "Let me tell you, I never believed in UFOs at all until I saw those kids. I mean, they couldn't possibly be from here. That's why I think they're something extraterrestrial. They come down here and pretend to be kids but it comes off creepy, they don't have it right yet."

Looking over the cases of BEK encounters gives one the sense that a grand experiment is taking place. Accounts follow similar patterns, yet there are constant, slight variations. Is some master manipulator tweaking the system behind the scenes? Some researchers place the Men in Black in a broader context of the mysterious. Folklorist Thomas E. Bullard writes:

"Almost a sense of familiarity attaches to the Men in Black. They step into the shoes vacated by angels and demons to serve as modernized versions of other-worldly messengers, modified to reflect extraterrestrial rather than supernatural employment but clearly functionaries in the same mold."

This description could easily fit encounters with the black eyed children. Such viewpoints offer an interesting perspective. Mysterious figures in black have shown up through history. In early times, they were associated with religious or occult movements. Later, the MIB showed up when UFO sightings and Contactees became the buzzwords of the day. Perhaps the sudden increase in black eyed kid encounters is the modern expression of this unknown force.

BEKs, MIB, UFOs, somehow perhaps they do all fit together in some fortean mosaic of the weird.

Whatever they are, the black eyed children don't appear to be going anywhere and they are leaving as many questions in their wake as the MIB before them. Whether the two are connected or not, it looks like we're in for more bizarre manifestations ahead. So pay attention. The next time there's a knock at your door, there's no telling what kind of strange figure is calling.

Sources:

Bullard, Thomas E. *UFO Abductions: The Measure of a Mystery. Volume 1: Comparative Study of Abduction Reports. Volume 2: Catalogue of Cases.* Mount Rainer, MD: Fund for UFO Research, 1987.

Keel, John A. *The Mothman Prophecies.* New Yor, NY: Saturday Review Press/E.P. Dutton and Company, 1975.

Redfern, Nick. *The Real Men In Black.* Pompton Plains, NJ: New Page Books, 2011.

4.

"I noticed a kind of change in the air, a shift, a weird shift"

Peter Beckman is, to put it mildly, an intriguing character. Having grown up in Northern California, as a youngster he gravitated towards the arts and acting and was soon involved with local theater and production companies.

In his early twenties, Peter attended the California Institute of Arts, where he studied screenwriting alongside Alexander Mackendrick of *The Man in the White Suit* fame. His movie appearances include *Chud II*, Orson Welles' unfinished *The Other Side of the Wind*, and *Echo Park*.

Beckman is the voice of General Wolf in the SyFy Channel's series, Monster; he worked as a voice-artist on *Street Fighter 4* and *5*, *Dissidia, the Final Fantasy*, and many other video games; and is the author of a highly entertaining paranormal-themed novel, *Dead Hollywood*.

In addition, Beckman is the male voice in Josie Cotton's recordings of *Beyond the Valley of the Dolls*, and *Faster Pussycat, Kill! Kill!* And, if like me you're a big fan of the Ramones, you'll be interested to know that Peter had a starring role in the video for the band's 1983 single, *Psycho Therapy*, in which he receives a kicking in the head, courtesy of a psychotic punk-rocker!

Peter is also someone who had a deeply weird run-in with the MIB, a story he shared after he heard me on *Coast to Coast* with George Noory, in 2011, talking about my book, *The Real Men in Black*. In Peter's very own words…

I'm pretty much a regular listener to *Coast to Coast* and the night you were on I happened to be tuning in. I have always been fascinated by the MIB legend; I had read about Albert Bender. But I had never really connected it with the experience I had back in 1969 or 1970 - when I would have been about 20 or 21 - until you described a sequential series of events that are common, and you practically described what happened to me.

There was a friend with me at the time, Stephen Leeson, and we had taken mescaline at like 1.00 or 2.00 p.m. in the afternoon. Carmichael, California is where I lived, a small town northeast of Sacramento. Our house was on a private road, off the main drag in Carmichael, which was Fair Oaks Boulevard. This was my parents' house, but they were gone for a few days, so we pretty much had the place to ourselves.

By about 9.00 or 10.00 p.m. the mescaline had pretty much worn off. We had a joint or two in the living-room, but not much more than that. The living room was an A-frame, 14-feet-tall in the center. It had huge picture-windows, front and aft. You could see the road through the front window.

We were big movie fans and great fans of Roman Polanski's movies. We loved *The Fearless Vampire Hunters* and *Rosemary's Baby*. Stephen had a brother that was, I think, program-director at one of the TV channels and they had 16mm prints in their library, like *Repulsion* and *Cul-de-sac*. So, Stephen would bring them over to watch. We used to go to the drive-in movies in Steve's 1956 Cadillac hearse!

This night we were listening to the soundtrack to *Rosemary's Baby* by Krzysztof Komeda. As one of the tracks ended, I noticed a kind of change in the air, a shift, a weird shift. It was a change in the mood of the place. And then the black mass track came on. Then things really changed. It seemed to me like we were in my living-room, but also some place else.

In the southwest corner of the room was a dining table, which was overhung by a large lamp, on a chain, about 9 or 10 feet off the ground. We both saw the lamp change into a large, black-hooded figure. There were, it seemed to me, 2 or 3 of them, and the other two were standing a few feet in back of the main one. And we were like locked in place, staring at them. I don't remember seeing any eyes or anything. Then suddenly nothing; they were gone.

We looked at each other and it was like: What the fuck was that? It was incredible. I first put it all down to hallucination, but then I heard you on the show and I thought: well, maybe, it *wasn't* a hallucination. I'd taken LSD and been around the psychedelic scene in San Francisco, and pretty much knew the difference between reality and being under the influence of LSD. By this time, the album had ended.

Now, no one ever comes up that road, hardly ever unless you lived there, were a guest or a friend, and especially at that time of morning. We were more than surprised to see bright lights coming up the road and shining through the Monterrey pine at the edge of the property. They were so bright they were almost like theatrical lights. I thought it was one of our neighbors, but all of a sudden the lights went off.

We could make out the car, and it was long, like a stretch, black limo. Then a door opened and shut. I don't know how long we waited, but we waited for a while for a knock at the front-door, but it never came. Several minutes – maybe 5 or 6 – the limo, or whatever it was, proceeded around the road.

I remember asking Steve to go to the west side of the house, which was my father's painting studio, to watch it go by. I went to my bedroom, in the east end of the house to look out the window. Steve never saw anything go by, and I never saw anything go by. We had also lost some time: the Sun was coming up. All through this time I couldn't see my dog, a poodle, and finally found him under my bed, which he had never done before.

`Now, as you continued talking with George [Noory], a memory came back. At least, it feels like a memory, part of which has come back. There *was* a knock at the door. I remember the knock at the front door. I don't recall if it was me or Steve who said: 'Better let them in.' I opened it; we admitted two men into the house. After what we had just seen, in retro-spect this seems amazing.

They were pretty much as you described on *Coast to Coast*: they were dressed in square, Eisenhower-era cop-clothing, or FBI clothing – which in 1969 or 1970 was not that unusual. They came in and sat on the couch. They were pale and sickly; their clothes hung *real* loose and they looked as though they might expire at any moment. They appeared to have either trouble breathing, or trouble even *being*. I don't believe they said a thing. If they did, it has disappeared from memory. Very odd, indeed.

I recall that, as I was waiting for them to speak, my mind was racing; should I try humor or invective? My general impression is that they were kind of confused, but just ever so slightly amused by the situation. It was as though they were waiting for us to speak. Their physical attitudes seemed to be waiting for some sort of answer, although no questions were asked. We were all waiting.

This frightened me for an instant; then the whole scene felt absurd and humorous.

After a couple of minutes, I started feeling funny about this, and I started saying something like: "Can we see some ID? Did someone send you? What are you really here for?" But this did not affect them at all. When I thought: "I want them to leave," they seemed to pick up on this, and *did* leave. This had to have been between the time when we first saw the lights and looked for them when the car left.

It is important to remember that our private road went around our acre in a square-shape; once the limo pulled up front, there was literally *no way* for it to turn around; it *had to* follow the road in order to leave, but Steve and I never saw it do so, and we *looked*! Now it seems to me that the reason we didn't see it is that the MIB episode was blocked from our minds immediately after it had occurred, so that all we saw was the limo stop, the door open and close, the limo proceeding along the road. Then we spread out to look for it, not realizing we had lost time (the meeting with the MIB.)

For years, that part of it was locked away. But listening to the show brought it out. In all the time I took psychedelics, which is probably around 150 times, this is the only time I have had an experience like that.

5.

"My encounter with an 'old Man in Black'"

The following account, from Terry – in Shingle Springs, California – is without doubt one of the most chilling MIB-themed reports ever to have reached me. Read on and you'll see why…

This encounter occurred during the day time thirty five years ago in 1977 at a Winchell's in Sunnyvale, California, I was just sixteen years of age at the time. My best friend and I had just finished our coffee and were heading for the doorway to leave. As we were passing a man seated at one of the tables, he reached out and firmly grabbed my wrist. In that moment, my first reaction was to jerk away from his grip, but looking down at him I realized that he was a very old man and I felt in that moment that he was harmless. He was dressed in black, wearing an old fashioned hat and suit, his clothing looked like it was from the 1930's. He was extremely pale, very thin and appeared to be very old, I guessed in his 80's or 90's.

He told my friend and I that he was a palm reader, a very good one, he claimed. Could he please do us a favor by giving us each a reading? My friend and I talked briefly to each other about his offer and agreed to let him. I first sat down across the table from him, then as my friend was starting to sit down along side of me, he stopped her and asked her to please go sit a few tables away out of earshot from us, explaining that the information was going to be direct and personal, we would need some privacy. She complied and moved several tables away.

Once my friend was seated away from the us, I placed my hands on the table in front of him, palms up and looked into the man's face. I then noticed the old man's eyes were completely glazed over with cataracts, he was surely blind, I thought, as his gaze was unfixed and unfocused in my direction. I asked him how long had he been a psychic? He responded by saying that his ability had nothing to do with being psychic and emphasized that it had everything to do with "science".

He began by talking about my early childhood experiences along with some very painful incidents. He had precise and detailed information that I was sure no one could have known about. Quite suddenly I felt very vulnerable and exposed as he recounted these events, his knowledge unnerved me to my very core. Staring straight ahead, he moved along into my present situation, lecturing and chastising me like a father would a child, for some poor choices I had made during that time. All the while he broke a doughnut down into tiny pieces. My mind raced as I tried to figure out how on earth could he know this stuff? It was then in that moment that I would forever change my ideas of "secrets kept" and how I viewed my own identity in the world. Apparently "nothing" could be hidden from myself or anyone else for that matter. I felt naked in the truth.

He continued this reading, now delving into my future and that of upcoming world events, with stories sometimes so harsh and brutal that I clearly remember wondering if I would ever "catch a break in life?" Among other things, he warned me of a time when that by speaking about my UFO experiences I would anger "the governmental powers that be" and he cautioned that I would be dealing with very dangerous people and circumstances. He rambled on often emphasizing again that this all had to do with "science."

I then asked him if he could see any kind of success coming to me, ever?

He responded by telling me, "You will not find success in life, you will die of a broken heart. It will be a better stronger woman who will be successful."

As I listened to his words I began to cry and he sharply asked me, "Are you going to lay down and die like a frightened whore, or are you going to be willing to stand up and fight like a worthy warrior?" I was stunned into silence and then he said, "Whether you realize this or not, I have done you a huge favor today and I will be returning to see you in the future, ___ years from now to collect on it."

As a side note, I do not recall the exact time he said, but do recall thinking "You'll be long dead by then old man". Our reading ended, he asked me to leave the table and he then waived for my friend to come over to sit with him. He spent all of five minutes with her and when she arose from the table she was badly shaken and would only say that she hoped that what he predicted for her was not true.

As we exited the doughnut shop I tried to press my friend for more information because she was crying, but she was too upset to speak about what he had said to her. Once out on the street the both of us walking together toward home, my friend asked me to tell her about what the old man said to me in my reading with him, she pointed out that the reading he gave went on for an hour and forty five minutes with me.

I was lost for words when she spoke up and said, "Linda I don't think he was a person, I think that old man was an alien."

Right in that moment as she was speaking, we watched as an old black 1930's or 40's gangster type car with running boards pull out of the parking lot and pass us on the street. There was no driver at the wheel and the same old man that we had met was riding in the back seat. Our mouths dropped as we watched the car pass by us and at the same time a whirlwind picked up and swirled around our feet. We watched the car disappear from view making a turn further down the street.

I then shook my head and responded to her with "No, he was just a creepy old man in black."

Over the years during the course of our friendship, my friend and I would ponder and question our meeting with "the old man in black" many times. We could not understand who or what he was and neither of us would reveal to the other exactly what his frightening messages to each of us separately were, agreeing only that we felt that he was speaking the truth and that it was frightening for both us. We would part ways and our friendship ended in 1988 when I came out to her about my lifelong UFO experiences and the old man's messages to me. She mocked and ridiculed me in that moment. It was a very painful ending to our relationship for me; I would struggle with it for years.

In 1988 when I began to seriously study the UFO phenomena I came across stories about these Men in Black, Master Tricksters and the like. It was then that I began to understand who and what they are and how this "old man in black" specifically related to me as that young teenager all those years ago and yet, I was still haunted by his promise to return to collect on that favor.

During Christmas of 2009, alone in my mother's apartment while she traveled, I found myself slipping into a deep depression and I was filled with despair. During the course of that year I had lost a job that I loved due to the economy, gone through a terrible break up with a man I could no longer love. I found out that my old friend who was with me in 1977 on that day with the "old man in black" in Sunnyvale had died in 2008 from cancer and I had still not gotten over losing my beloved horse Meaghan, who had also died the year before, leaving me filled with a sorrow that I was not able to overcome.

Starting on Christmas Day, I fasted and prayed for three

days hoping that I could find some peace and comfort. I realized that, I was indeed "heart broken" over my losses and suddenly the encounter with "the old man in black" came flooding back into my mind and would not leave me alone. In trying to escape his words and his terrible messages to me, I began drinking heavily at night until I could find some peace in sleep. This would go on into the beginning of 2011 when I finally began to slowly recover from the pain. I finally thought I had come to terms with that old man's warnings and I successfully quit drinking. My attitude shifted and I was now looking forward to a great new year.

In April of last year, I discovered a lump in my breast and was at first unconcerned about it, I thought that it was probably a just a fibroid cyst that would go away on its own. I put off having it checked out until July when the lump had grown quite large and when the results came back positive for cancer, I was shocked. Last month after trying a lot of alternative therapies in the prior months since July, I had a mastectomy. The pathology indicates that I have advanced stage cancer and once again the "old man in black" and his words are haunting me. Oddly I find myself both eager and apprehensive as I await his return, but know that above all, I am no longer afraid.

There is one final, very strange story to tell. Terry emailed the above account to me on February 28, 2012. In the copy that arrived, after the final sentence above that ends "…I am no longer afraid," were these words: "I will probably have to keep him at bay when he returns."

When I sent Terry's text back to her, to show her how it would be formatted in the pages of this book, she replied that she did not write those words of "I will probably have to keep him at bay when he returns."

Rather, the last words in the email Terry sent me stated that with respect to the old MIB, she "would embrace him warmly."

In other words, the email she sent me was subtly different to the one I received. To this day, neither Terry nor I have been able to explain how such an odd, and somewhat unsettling, change should have been made to her text.

The bigger questions, of course, are: (a) who was responsible for making the change? and (b) why?

6.

"The MIB seem just a little off"

From writer and filmmaker Sean Kotz we have a truly fascinating observation on the Men in Black and their curious characteristics…

Observations and Theories on the MIB Phenomenon
– By Sean Kotz

A disclaimer: I feel compelled, because of the nature of the coming observation and the highly speculative scenarios presented below, to let readers know that I understand this might be disturbing or offensive. That is not my intention. Please be aware that I make absolutely no judgments here and write with the goal of balancing clarity with sensitivity. If I have failed, especially regarding readers for whom this might hit close to home, it is not because I have been indifferent and I apologize.

An observation: One of the things that makes the Man in Black phenomenon so fascinating is the general social oddity of encounters. In everything from displaced fashions, to mechanical grammar and outdated expressions, to trying to drink Jello or fixating on ashtrays and ink pens, the MIB seem just a little off.

These qualities have led some to conclude that the MIB are extraterrestrials, time travelers, or inter-dimensional observers on specific missions requiring that they gather information without raising suspicion, but are ultimately unable to fit in because they are essentially not of this world. However, in most cases, the strange behavior does have an earthly parallel, an increasingly common disorder frequently classed as a form of high functioning autism called Asperger's Syndrome.

Asperger's Syndrome, or AS, was first formally identified by Austrian physician Hans Asperger in 1944 and has since become a formally recognized disorder, frequently classed as a form of high functioning autism. Both autism in general and AS in particular can appear in a wide range of severity and in some very mild cases, almost impossible to identify. Indeed, Asperger's Syndrome can exhibit some remarkably heightened skill sets and IQs, which may present evidence of a contemporary genetic evolution of our species.

But before we can make any speculations as to why that might be, we should consider how deeply this connection runs.

Trademarks of Asperger's Syndrome: According to WebMD and ASPEN (Asperger's Syndrome Education Network), the overriding identifier with AS is difficulty or even inability to recognize social cues, especially non-verbal social cues, creating awkward interactions with others. They may either avoid eye contact altogether or stare directly at another person. They may fail to recognize or properly interpret body language or understand personal space. AS individuals typically display naivety or flat out obliviousness regarding this awkwardness, which can make children the victims of bullies or predators and promote isolation as well.

Not surprisingly then, people with AS have trouble with the give and take of normal conversation. They are inclined to engage in highly focused, inordinately detailed one-sided dialogues with people and have trouble shifting gears in conversation or letting go of a train of thought. However, once they have exhausted their knowledge or interest in a topic, they can stop a conversation abruptly. They may also verbalize internal thoughts freely, not realizing the impact of such things on others.

Additionally, people with Asperger's Syndrome have trouble grasping humor, sarcasm, metaphor, colloquialisms, intonation, and other subtleties of language. Instead, they incline to very literal interpretations and tend to speak formally, using stilted but precise language, sometimes with words or phrases that seem out of time and place.

Another trait is that AS children have trouble developing fine motor skills and may have poor handwriting and experience difficulty learning to use a knife, fork or spoon. They exhibit awkward postures, often holding their bodies in seemingly uncomfortable rigidity or straightness. They may be relatively clumsy and have trouble with hand-eye coordination and they will frequently show a tendency toward tight fitting formal clothing. And, they may show sensitivity to light, noise and tastes or smells and do not like a disruption in routine or changes of plans.

On the other hand, people with Asperger's can show great abilities when it comes to memorization and pattern recognition. Interestingly enough, many people with AS often have high IQs and are drawn to astronomy, paleontology, architecture, engineering and other sciences. They may also a vast amount of arcane or obscure knowledge, develop a huge vocabulary, and display a keen interest in maps.

In a word, AS people are masters of "form." They dress and speak formally to the point of awkwardness. Their minds can catalogue names, dates, words, forms, formulas, and so forth with amazing recall and ease. In essence, Asperger's seems to give people a heightened awareness of form and structure, though ironically, there seems to be an exchange when it comes to fluidity and depth of perception.

Comparisons with the Men in Black: If you are already versed in MIB lore, many of these trademarks will seem familiar. I am not about to suggest that Men in Black are actually people with Asperger's, but the similarities are striking.

In a typical MIB encounter, witnesses describe men wearing crisp and clean black suits and shoes, white shirts and black ties that are generally out of date by several decades.

They arrive in black sedans that may also be shiny and new, but more than a generation old. Fashion distinctions escape people with AS and they might easily reason that a suit and tie and sedan lend formal respectability while not being able to distinguish the awkwardness of items out of time.

The MIB also frequently wear sunglasses even at night, which would both reduce the ill effects of light and help them avoid eye contact or disguise a tendency to stare. They will stand or sit rigidly and seem unaware of social protocols, missing cues to sit down or relax.

In conversation, MIB will frequently be focused on obscure details and refuse to stray from the subject. They will ask awkward and inappropriate questions without emotion, speak in robotic and overly formal ways and use words or phrases that seem out of time or place, though technically correct. All of this echoes the tendencies of Asperger's Syndrome.

In addition, MIB are often attributed with awkward gaits and strange ways of holding common items, like pens or forks. In one of John Keel's cases, a MIB ordered a steak in a restaurant only to be unable to use the cutlery. Also, MIB are known for having inappropriate reactions to the point of fixation with commonplace items like ballpoint pens.

In the well known case of Dr. Herbert Hopkins, a male and seemingly female pair visited him and his wife and proceeded to ask questions regarding their lives as a couple and even attempted a clumsy, mechanical show of affection, asking for directions as they went. The behavior is inexplicable in any case, but it displays both the inability to understand the inappropriateness of the behavior and the questions.

Perhaps the only thing that haunts the scorched ground of the paranormal more than its specters and aliens are the raging debates. Currently, one of the rifts in the esoteric community that divides researchers into two territories might be understood as a clash between Newtonian realists and quantum speculators.

On one hand, we have what Nick Redfern calls the "nuts and bolts" interpretation, which holds that UFOs are physical constructions (typically from another planet), Bigfoot is an elusive simian, and the Men in Black are either government agents or flesh and blood aliens dispatched on a mission to control witnesses, contactees and abductees. These interpretations rely on common sense physics and reflect the influence of scientific method and cause-and-effect rationalism in our culture.

On the other hand, since John Keel, it has become more and more acceptable to theorize the paranormal with terms like "interdimensional," "ultradimensional," and so forth. Pretty soon people are talking about reality matrixes, vortexes, and portals, which begins to sound like 19th Century pontifications on ectoplasm and spirit boxes. However, for the last half century, equally non-rational science has emerged to lend some degree of credence to these possibilities.

One of the most basic quantum principles that plagues both types of science and the paranormal investigator equally is the problem of observer interactivity. In other words, in every experiment, the observer (be it a scientist in a Harvard lab with two million dollar measurement tools or a pseudo-scientist in a haunted house with a K2 meter) becomes part of the environment and this affects, even if slightly, the results.

Additionally, we all bring our preconceived notions to the table as well. Consider for instance that in the late 1800s, people were reporting strange encounters with bizarre airships and their crews. Later, after Kenneth Arnold said the craft he saw flew like saucers skipping over water, the term "flying saucer" took hold and suddenly, that is what people began to see. In the enough, something like the star destroyers seen in *Star Wars*.

I mention all this because it may be helpful in understanding the Men in Black phenomenon. Perhaps, the MIB are both very real but entirely subject to the conditions of the observer. For example, if you stand at the shore on a sunny day and look out at the ocean, it might look green, blue, gray, or totally light reflective depending on weather conditions and the time of day. And if you look at night, the waves will be black. The water certainly exists, and a given description may be very accurate at a specific time and place, but still the description of the water and the water itself are two very different things.

7.

"Something is wrong with this man – dangerously wrong"

In his own words, "Jason Offutt's books include the paranormal titles, *What Lurks Beyond, Darkness Walks: Shadow People Among us, Haunted Missouri,* and *Paranormal Missouri,* the collection of humor essays *On Being Dad,* a humorous travelogue *Through a Corn-Swept Land:* an epic beer run through the Upper Midwest, and an upcoming zombie novel, *The Killing.*

His articles on the paranormal can be found at http://mysteriousuniverse.org. Jason lives with his family in Missouri where he teaches college journalism, and keeps humanity safe from the forces of evil…

....

The Hat Man and MIBs – By Jason Offutt

....

A dark figure lurks in the shadows, watching. Something about him is out of place. The Humphrey Bogart suit? The dark obscured features? Or maybe it's the hat. Not a ball cap, not a driving cap, but a fedora. This figure looks like it stepped from a 1940s detective magazine. Then it raises a hand, or takes a step; its movements awkward, exaggerated. Something is wrong with this man – dangerously wrong. This description, of a man in an out-of-date suit wearing an out-of-date hat, is common in the paranormal field, stretching across the line of the UFO-fixated Men in Black, and the darker, more shadowy Hat Man.

Men in Black, first reported in author and UFO researcher Gray Barker's 1956 book, "They Knew Too Much About Flying Saucers," are described as thin men, often exhibiting behavior that doesn't fit with society. They wear sunglasses, old fashioned black suits or out-of-place clothing, and harass people who have UFO encounters. Some MIBs confront abductees as government agents, others claim to be aliens, and still others just make their presence known.

Gil once worked as a guard at the now-decommissioned state penitentiary in Jefferson City, Missouri, and has tried for years to convince the world the former prison is a hub of UFO activity.

"I've seen so many UFOs," he said. One night calling bingo in nearby Columbia, Missouri, three strange men walked into the game room and stared at Gil.

"All were dressed in black suits," he said. "All were about the same size. Same kind of shirt, same kind of tie." And they wore the same hat. Gil soon lost them in the crowd. During cleanup, Gil asked if anyone had seen these men; no one had. But Gil knew he'd seen the Men in Black for one reason – they wanted him know they were watching.

This type of Men in Black encounter is typical, but what of the Hat Man? An entity that's features are masked in shadow, its appearance often described as two-dimensional, like a peel-off sticker on a child's cheap dollhouse?

Like the Men in Black, the Hat Man has floated in the periphery of our lives for decades, observing our movements, occasionally interacting with us, but always threatening. Charles was 13 years old in 1949 and lived with his mother, brother and grandmother in San Jose, California, when the Hat Man crept into his life. He lay in bed with his brother, talking before they drifted off to sleep, when the window sash moved.

"A dark figure dressed in a black cloak and wearing a black hat with a wide brim appeared in the window," Charles said. "No facial features were discernible on this person, but I took it to be a man."

This Hat Man opened the window and reached through with both hands.

"I thought he was going to climb in," Charles said. "At that moment I started yelling my head off." As Charles's young voice pierced the night, the Hat Man closed the window, turned and disappeared from sight. The next morning, Charles saw the window was locked from the inside. "I saw something," Charles said. "What in the hell was it?"

People have reported the Hat Man from England to Brazil, Australia to California. From eyewitness reports, this entity can be solid or vapor, a waking nightmare or a sleep disorder, a real entity or the result of electric stimulation to the brain. Because the Hat Man is described as more ethereal than Men in Black, there are many possible explanations as to whether these are entities, or something psychological.

Sleep Paralysis: Hormones in REM sleep paralyze the major muscle groups. When people suddenly wake, the hormones stay in their bodies for up to eight minutes. During this time they can feel pressure on their chest and can see people that seem real. This feeling, also known as "Old Hag Syndrome," and according to psychology, is fairly common.

Archetype: Since the first black and white gangster movies, the media has programmed us to fear figures in dark suits and fedoras, so in the dim silence of the night, a coat rack in an unfamiliar room may appear to us as a Hat Man.

Tricking the brain: Electronic stimuli to certain sections of the brain, and tricks of light and shadow have been shown by scientific testing to make people see this dark figure.

Ghosts: Many paranormal investigators and psychics consider the Hat Man to be nothing more than the earthbound spirits reflecting their appearance in life.

Demons: According to a Catholic exorcist, demons can manifest themselves in the form of this shadowy entity, sometimes with glowing red eyes, as some Hat Men are described having.

Omens: The Hat Man is also associated with impending doom. People have reported seeing a Hat Man looming in the shadows before the onset of some tragedy, such as an accident, a major disaster, or a death.

Dimensional travelers: Some speculate that Hat Men are observing us from other dimensions, their shadow persona being only our perception of what these people look like in their own world.

Extraterrestrials: A growing number of people are placing the Hat Man into the realm of extraterrestrial contact because of the similarities in the encounters, such as silently entering bedrooms at night, paralyzing those who see them, and sometimes feeding upon their energy. These entities, like ET encounters, seem to visit the same people time after time.

People like Cody.
The Cowboy has followed Cody for years, a black, human-shaped figure, featureless except for a hat – a fedora with a wide brim. Cody spent most of his childhood cowering under the covers as this Hat Man paced through the bedroom he shared with his brother.

"We called him the Cowboy because he kind of looked like the Marlboro man," Cody said. The visits stopped during Cody's senior year in high school; then in 2011 the Cowboy returned.

"My car started acting up," he said. "I'm in the process of looking for a job, finding an apartment, buying an engagement ring. I had a lot of stuff on my plate, which might have brought on what happened."

What happened was the Cowboy.

"I'm sitting in my car on the phone with my mom," Cody said. As he described the car's behavior to his mother, he noticed a movement in the corner of his right eye. Cody turned toward the passenger side window and saw it – the shadow man that tormented him in the night as a child.

"It was full on. A shadow person in an old fedora," Cody said. "It was standing there. It leaned over like it's bending to look at me." As Cody stared in horror, the Cowboy reached out its arm and knocked on the car window. "It knocked two times," Cody said. "After it knocked it dissolved in my vision. It just showed up, knocked on my window and was gone." Cody wonders if the Cowboy wanted to let him know it was still around. "It's been quite some time since I saw him," he said. "I was feeling stressed out and I think he showed up just to feed on that."

Given the reports, Men in Black and the Hat Man are likely related only in casual appearance. The dark suit, the fedora, the awkward movements. But where Men in Black talk, the Hat Man is silent. Men in Black appear within the norm of humanity (if not slightly pale, waxy, and thin), the Hat Man appears two-dimensional, showing no features, just a deep, black silhouette. Men in Black are reported to appear at the doorstep of UFO witnesses, the Hat Man appears to anyone, at any time. These entities have similarities, but if they're related, it's only by their great taste in hats.

8.

"There was nothing friendly about the way he was grinning."

"Christine" grew up in West Texas and was confronted on more than a few occasions by one of the weirdest and creepiest offshoots of the MIB mystery – namely, the so-called "Grinning Man…"

I haven't told a lot of people about it. When I first saw the person, I was about 1 or 2 years old. I have a very long memory. It was like the typical thing that you hear: it was this man who would stand in the doorway of my bedroom. I remember standing up in my crib and holding onto the bars and looking at him: He wore a fedora and a tan raincoat and black trousers, shiny shoes and black leather gloves. His face wasn't like someone who had been burned, but he just stood there and would grin. There was nothing friendly about the way he was grinning. It was horrible. Emotionless, didn't blink. And he came off and on for a few years.

Even as I got older and slept in my own bed, I would wake up sometimes, like at 3 o'clock in the morning, and that went on. That still happens: all of a sudden I'll be wide awake at 3 o'clock in the morning, for no apparent reason. But as a kid, I'd wake up at 3 o'clock and he'd be there. I didn't have any frame of reference for it. Of course, my mom didn't believe me; she just thought I was dreaming.

But there were all sorts of strange paranormal things that happened throughout my childhood and I wonder if it was all part of the same thing. I even got weird phone calls as a teenager. The phone would ring and it sounded like a little kid speaking in another language; just rapidly talking into the phone. I thought at the time it was some little kid got on a payphone and started dialing numbers from another country. But, when I read *The Mothman Prophecies*, I went: Holy shit! This was the same thing.

What validated that this person was real was that when I was twelve, a friend and I were out riding our bikes about 9.30 at night in the summer – it was a small town in west Texas. And we stopped and were looking in the doors of the Baptist church, as they had just put in new carpets. A big Saturday night! But, we both turned at the same time to look behind us and this man appeared like right on the edge of the street light and started walking towards us, and he was wearing the exact same outfit: the fedora and the tan overcoat and black pants. But, this time, his whole head and hands were bandaged. We didn't speak; we just took off like a shot, around the corner, to her house. We didn't know what to make of it, but I thought it was probably that same person that I used to see. I've never seen him again.

When I got into my early twenties, I was living in Dallas and I met a girl; we got to talking about paranormal stuff and she lived in Lufkin, in east Texas. She said that she and her sister shared a room and that sometimes she would wake up and there would be this man in her room. She said he wore a hat and a long coat. He reminded her of the McDonald's "Hamburglar" and he would just stand there grinning at her. One night, she woke up and he was looking at her, but he was petting her sister's head while she slept.

And then, a few years later, another friend of mine who had grown up in New York, said she had seen a similar man and that he would stand in her room. I thought, okay that's great; I am absolutely not nuts. I had lights that would turn off and on. My stuff got moved around all the time. I still have my things get moved around. I had a poster of Marilyn Monroe jump off my wall. It was like 6 o'clock, I think I was sixteen, and it just flew off the wall and into middle of the floor. I grew up in a really religious family: Southern Baptist; so that was all something of the Devil, although I don't believe that now.

There was another visible entity that used to show up. It was black, sort of shapeless, but had these enormous eyes, kind of like the quintessential way we depict aliens. The great big eyes were silvery with no pupil. They had a reflective quality. Again, it would be 3 o'clock in the morning and I would feel my bed jolt. I would look down and see those eyes, right over the edge of my bed, and the black shapelessness around it.

I turned on the light once I got my courage up. I thought:

if I don't move it's going to kill me, and if I do move it's going to kill me. Again, I was sixteen or seventeen. I screamed for my mom. I just told her I had a nightmare. But then I saw it again; one morning I was getting ready to go to school. I turned toward the shower and I could see the eyes looking between the hooks on the shower curtain.

The final time this thing appeared, I didn't see it. I had a friend sleeping over, a senior in high-school. She had never been to my house and I had never told her about any of this kind of stuff. She was very religious; didn't really believe in any of this or would have said it was the Devil.

We were up the next morning, and she was helping me make my bed and I said: "It was a lot of fun; you should come back over."

She looked at me and said: "I'm sorry, I'm never gonna come back here."

I said: "What did I do?"

She said: "You didn't do anything. How do you not remember?"

I said: "I really don't know what you're talking about; you'll have to tell me."

She said she woke up suddenly during the night and she thought that she couldn't see. Then, when her eyes adjusted, there was a face so close to hers that she couldn't see anything else. I asked her what it looked like and she said the same thing: these big eyes and just black. She said she screamed so loud she figured she woke the whole neighborhood.

All I did, according to her, was lift up and sit up on my elbow and look at her and said: "Are you okay?"

She said she was and went back to sleep. My mom didn't hear it either. And, sure enough, she never came back to my house.

I did have a person who would actually call me and talk to me while I was in high-school. It may have just been some nut, but he seemed to know everywhere that I went. I took dance classes in Abilene and I had friends that lived there as well.

This person would call late at night and ask: "How was your dance class?"

He knew my every move, which was odd. They wouldn't tell me who they were. They knew a week's worth of my activities. I might have decided to see a friend and not had those plans prior. So, no one would know where I was going, but this person knew where I had been.

The last time I saw him was in a dream when I was thirteen and it was a lucid dream. I was in a store, looking at a rack of magazines. I turned and looked to my left and there he was. He had a magazine in his hand and he was staring right at me and grinning. In the dream, I put my magazine down and I walked right past him and told him: "Don't ever come here again." And he never did. That was the last time I saw him, physically or in a dream. I just decided, right there, in my dream, I'm not having this anymore.

I know that when I do think about him it does spur

activity in my house; when I look into it again or the paranormal. I wonder how much of that is energy that I'm putting out. I never had any sightings of UFO phenomena attached to it.

Oh, there was one thing: I was driving home from Abilene one night – and there is an Air Force base there – and I saw apparently an aircraft, although there were no lights on it. But it left a green, glowing vapor behind it and it was traveling really, really fast. But it could have been some kind of Air Force thing.

9.

"You will not discuss
what happened"

Denise Stoner is the Director of the Florida Research Group affiliation of UFORCOP, a MUFON National Abduction Research Team (ART) member, a Florida MUFON Field Investigator, a Star Team Member, and a former Florida MUFON, State Section Director, and Chief Investigator. She co-authored and published her first book *The Alien Abduction Files*, which released in May of 2013.

She also holds educational forums for public and private gatherings for abduction experiencers. Her involvement in the UFO field spans more than 25 years. Denise has an educational background in business and psychology, and is a certified hypnotist specializing in regressive hypnosis. She has taught classes in stress reduction for 12+ years for professionals in such fields as medicine and law.

She began her research in hypnosis under Dr. Bob Romack, (Denver, CO). They worked together for five years on pain control, smoking cessation, and past life regression research.

For 12 years Denise did back ground investigations for

the military on recruits seeking highly classified clearances for work on nuclear submarines. Prior to retirement, Denise moved to the Naval Air Warfare Center, Training Systems Division, military research facility where she was the training coordinator for several hundred military and civilian employees.

She is a retired S.C.U.B.A. instructor, cave diver and former research member of the National Speleological Society Cave Diving Section. Her "retirement" from the Federal Government has allowed her to expand her work with UFO research and investigation. Denise has appeared on TV to include the Travel Channel, PBS, over 100 radio shows in 2012, and speaks yearly at the Daytona Museum of Arts and Science and the Paranormal Investigative Association, plus other venues.

She has worked as an on-camera expert for documentaries produced in the UK and she is currently moving forward with some exciting new projects such as her research on the commonalities among abductees now on its second study. Her Hypnotist certification came through Hypnosis & Regression Training at the Hypnotic Research Society by Dr. Ronald P. De Vasto. Advanced Regression study through the National Guild of Hypnotist, Inc. by Donald J. Mottin.

She has been invited to become a part of the newly formed Foundation for Research into Extraterrestrial Encounters (FREE) as a member of the research team. Denise can be contacted through her website at www.denisemstoner.com.

At least three times here in Florida at a particular combination health/grocery/restaurant called Whole Foods, I have been observed by a strange character. This is a good place to blend as many folks who shop here are "odd characters" to begin with or "hippie-like," gone back to nature types. So, the person who observed me was wearing a gauzy outfit, thin hair, woven straw Panama type hat and sun glasses and fit right in. His skin, hair, and clothing were all almost the same beige color.

The difference was he had a drink in front of him, a note-book and stared at me the whole time as we ate at a table on the sidewalk. He never had food of his own nor did he touch the drink. It seems he knew when we were almost fin-ished eating, he got up, walked slowly past our table, rounded the corner that was clearly visible but must pass a pillar on the corner of the shopping plaza by our table. Once he went behind that pillar, he never came out the other side. There was literally nowhere for him to go but out the other side, then down the sidewalk or out to the parking lot - but no, he was gone. I cannot get up to follow, thinking I am was going to bump in to him on the other side of the pillar. He let me know in no uncertain terms that he was watching me or letting me know he was there.

Yes, I have pondered many times what prevented me from picking up my cell phone and taking a picture of this individual. I have no answer for that. It absolutely crossed my mind the whole time the episode took place. Afterwards I feel foolish, knew I would be made fun of for telling the story, and promised myself I will have the camera ready the next time. It never happened. Are we somehow prevented from having photographic evidence needed as proof?

I do have several speaking engagements a year and have decided to add one of these odd stories each time as I feel people need to know this type of thing exists. Let them decide for themselves what they think. This is going on and that is a fact - the fact appears to be that we have some type of 'human' with unusual abilities living among the earthly beings and our only choice for now is to be observant, to watch and wait.

What other options do we have?

And Denise has yet another account to relate…

I would be glad to describe the situation to you as it has remained clear as crystal in my mind. As for my Mom, she knows something happened but it has gotten foggy and she doesn't know why, yet she recalls something happened that made her feel very uncomfortable.

My Mom and I had gone to the mall on Christmas Eve for a couple of last minute stocking stuffer type gifts. We actually knew what we wanted so parked outside J.C. Penney's on the side where those goods were. We went in and immediately noticed that in late afternoon, there were only a few shoppers. We picked out our gifts and got in line at the cashier in back of two other people. We could easily see the exit door and the sun in the parking lot, we were facing that way.

The glass doors opened and two very tall, thin women entered. They had long almost waist length blond hair parted in the middle on top and it was thin in texture. Their skin was also pale and I did not notice any make up but each had huge piercing blue eyes. Their gait was odd like they were too tall (approximately 6'1) to walk smoothly. I was already an investigator for MUFON so was aware of oddities in people and had done background searches for the Federal Government, so I was trained to be observant.

They were pushing one of those umbrella style strollers with no fancy attachments - just the hammock type bed, wheels, and handles. I noticed they had no purses or accessories such as a diaper bag to carry diapers or bottles. The women moved slowly it seemed and drew my attention to the stroller. There was a baby blanket in the bottom portion and on top the head of a baby no bigger than a small grapefruit, pasty colored skin, no noticeable nose, a line for a mouth and huge dark eyes taking up most of the rest of this head.

I wondered if the baby was deformed but knew this was not the case somehow. The baby appeared alert and was staring up at me.

My Mom bumped me with her arm to get my attention and said "what is wrong with that baby."

I felt I needed to tell the person in front of me because we had been talking (with her) about being slow in finishing up our shopping. When I tapped her on the shoulder, I then was shocked to see not only her but the lady in front of her and the cashier were kind of frozen in place. Everything seemed to be moving in extremely slow motion around us.

The blond women seemed to pass the thought to me that I needed to take another good look at the baby and study it. Then, as if a film was put back in to normal speed they walked past me and the cash register began to work, people - the only three in the area were moving again as if nothing happened.

I told my Mom to hold our places and I ran after the women. Just next to us was the infants' clothing department. The women had turned in to that aisle. I followed and when I turned in to the aisle - they disappeared. Just gone. Like they had never been there. I ran back the short distance to my Mom and told her they were gone.

We checked out and my Mom kept saying "what was going on with that baby?"

I told her no one goes shopping with a baby that tiny without taking needed supplies, bottles, diapers, clothes, etc.

I remember asking her if she thought we had seen something alien, such as a hybrid, and she just shook her head as if there was no answer. We stepped out the door and that's when the experience with the men took place.

When we exited the mall, my Mom had already stepped off the curb to locate my car. I was stopped by three men who were leaning on the brick wall by the door. Wearing black suits, black hats, white shirts, sunglasses. Short in stature. The only difference from your reports was the fact that one had a briefcase - black also. I don't recall their mouths moving but it could be I was just nervous.

One of them said, "you will not discuss what happened inside that store, do not talk about it to anyone, do you understand?"

I did not answer, stepped off the curb as I felt I was in danger and called after my Mom. Just after I stepped off the curb, I turned back to discover these men were gone. There was nowhere for them to go other than in to the parking lot or further down the sidewalk as there was a brick wall where they had been that continued down the length of the building to the only door we had come out.

We had been shown something in the store we both feel wasn't normal and were talking about it as we left. Were we imagining things when I met these men? Does this sound typical of these types? I am too old to be abducted and used for breeding and have had a hysterectomy so that could not have been the purpose - to show me a child of mine; I felt nothing like that was going on.

10.

"These MIB seem to be able to drain a person's energy"

Peter McMillan is retired, and from Ontario, Canada. He is a former chair and CEO of a computer sales and service corporation who graduated from Niagara College of Applied Arts and Technology in the field of electronics engineering. He is a former member of the Ontario Association of Certified Engineering Technicians and Technologists, a former member of the Institute of Electrical and Electronics Engineers, and someone who has personally experienced a great many phenomenon related to both paranormal and UFO activity. And here's Peter to tell you about his theories and thoughts on the MIB…

....

Modeling the Origins and Purpose of the Men in Black
– By Peter McMillan

....

The Judeo/Christian Bible reveals a lot about the different types of spirits that exist and the ways they can interact with us. My theory on the MIB is based on an understanding of just two classes of these spirits.

The Fallen Angels

Scriptures reveal that long ago a war took place in the heavens between rival factions of angelic beings. This war reached unto God's throne (called The Third Heaven) Who cast the opposing side (represented by Satan and his revolutionaries) into the abyss of outer space (called The Second Heaven) where they remain unto this day. Nothing prevents these defeated spirits from coming and going between our own planet and their settlements scattered throughout the universe. Whenever they visit earth they do so through cloud covered portals located within our own atmosphere (called The First Heaven).

The Demons

The Scriptures also relate how a hybrid race of beings, monstrous and gigantic in their sizes, strengths and abilities, flourished on the pre-flooded earth. These strange creatures were the result of a program of interbreeding between select members of the fallen angels and womankind. Angels often appeared to people in full physical form back then and their adopted forms were completely humanoid right down to fully functioning sexual organs and inheritable DNA.

It seems to be a general principle of life that anything born of human flesh can be occupied by a spirit (unlike the bodies of animals, mammals, plants or insects) and so each of these creatures must have contained a spirit. The Bible makes it clear that only the spirit of a physically dead human can return to God; so what about the spirits inhabiting these half angelic/half human hybrids?

I believe that upon physical death the spirits in these creatures would simply remain on the earth in a sort of twilight zone, being unable to return back to God or otherwise perish in any kind of eternal oblivion. The Bible refers to this race of disembodied spirits as demons. These creatures were never able to procreate themselves and it seems they all perished in the flood anyway. But even today they remain alive in the spiritual sense, completely conscious, and just as intelligent, powerful and resourceful as they ever were in material life; yet without any physical means of interacting with this world.

Bio-Engineered Bodies

Returning again to the notion that anything born of human flesh can be occupied by a spirit, it is conceivable that a sufficiently advanced medical technology could provide demons with bio-engineered replacement bodies grown in controlled laboratories from human tissue parts and DNA samples taken from already living specimens.

Fallen angels must have had such a continually developing technology at their disposal for centuries, seeing as we ourselves today within our own communities of medical scientists and genetic engineers can boldly lay claim to some of the very same patents. Demons are everywhere and know how to possess living tissue (presumably angels can only change into human form). Baiting these demons to occupy any suitably developed synthetic body that passes some kind of rigorous quality control testing would be academic for any angelic equivalent to a demon hunter/trapper.

This replacement technology and the constant need for fresh meat to clone could also help explain the purpose behind cattle mutilations and alien abduction experiments. Demonically hosted bio-engineered bodies complete with brain, nervous system, organs, muscles, speech apparatus, supporting skeleton and outer skin could then be specially trained and sent on special missions or remain more local as conscripted labor. I believe the reported alien greys that take part in abduction scenarios are one subset of these bio-engineered demon infested bodies.

The Men in Black

It has been reported that the MIB manifest very unusual physical forms, facial details and attire such as quasi-to-fully material bodies capable of extraordinary feats; short or wiry frames, white skin, bulging eyes, missing eyebrows or eyelashes, lipless mouths; and period clothing from a bygone era.

The Bodies

Available bio-engineered bodies might still have developmental problems at every stage in the growing process. As a practical engineering consequence of this, there might be severe height restrictions, frame volume and density considerations, and time and environmental constraints imposed on the useful "guaranteed" operation or life of any particular model. Running that model outside of its specific design parameters would noticeably and deleteriously affect the outward appearance, especially if there is a corruption or decay factor added to the equation.

As an example, follicle-rich skin which provides a scaffolding for the eyebrows may simply and randomly slide off such a body to expose a follicle-less layer beneath. As another example the wearing of lipstick on recently receded lip lines may be a way to compensate for an otherwise stark appearing mouth. As a final example the sometimes-reported bulging eyes could be a systemic problem associated with defects in a bio-engineered thyroid gland (or what passes for the thyroid). The also observed quasi-material or even ghostly-appearing states of some MIB can be accounted for by considering the very same technology that permits an observed UFO to suddenly appear, move or morph in defiance of natural physical laws, and finally blink out of existence. Today's frontier research scientists at MIT or elsewhere are already doing things like this with individual photons and tiny bits of real matter.

The Attire: Black Fedora Hats and Long Black Trench Coats
Imagine not having ever gone through growing stages from birth to toddler, adolescent, teenager, to young adult. These bio-engineered bodies come fully mature and ready to go right out of the box. The captured disembodied demon spirit crawls inside the baited body of flesh and starts to manipulate

it. Assuming that with any incarnation there is no prior memory of who or what it was before the demon might well ask the question "Who am I?"

Having been assigned period clothing for the purpose of its mission, this would also no doubt compensate for a lack of any real identity. I believe the MIB would desperately cling to that style of clothing for an entire lifetime, much like an insecure child might hold on to a security blanket.

"Who am I?" the MIB asks himself; "I am black fedora hat and black open collar trench coat. That is who I am and that is my identity!" When did the first MIB begin to appear (the 1940's) and what was the typical professional or business attire for men at that time (fedora hats and trench coats)? Fedora hats were very popular during a period from the 1920s to early 1950s. In fact, fedora hats and long trench coats worn together were widely preferred by men as a practical means of fully protecting the entire body from wind and weather. Any bio-engineered body would need insulation against the damaging environment at all times. Extreme photosensitivity to light (common among albinos) might also explain why some white skinned MIB wore sunglasses and drove black cars (they reduce reflected glare). The same can be said for their choice of color in clothing. The same line of thought regarding period cars and personal identity might also apply.

The Behavior

Many testimonies relate how odd these MIB appear to be in their conversation, walk, facial expressions, body language and other actions or movements. Our lives must be innately foreign to a demon. Originally these entities sprung forth as monstrous distortions of the flesh (before the flood). Their societies, ideologies, needs, desires, lusts and thoughts would have no parallel to our own. In their natural environment they would exhibit a behavior completely outside our ken. Demon slaves probably don't want to be told what to do by their fallen angelic masters anyway and therefore are likely to manifest both their "sent" behaviour as well as their natural default "demon-like" behavior at the same time. Just as with any highly trained monkey, these synthetic-fleshed demonically-possessed MIB would characteristically shift back and forth between what they were sent to do professionally by command and what they actually prefer to do by nature. Much of their odd behavior also seems to be similar to those with Asperger's Syndrome, perhaps another consequence of imperfect bio-engineering and/or a demon's natural behavior.

The Purpose

Why are most visitations of MIB limited to eyewitnesses of standard UFO sightings (an exception would be the case involving the Mothman prophecies)? Like psychic vampires, these MIB seem to be able to drain a person's energy and even break their will. Witnesses have reported being mentally confused, being in a dream-like state or even being probed telepathically. Regardless of these kinds of manifestations, all continue to report being both afraid and intimidated. I believe three things are going on here:

1. A kind of Stockholm Syndrome induced by the emotion of fear or awe, pleasurable (if not disturbing) sensory and psychological cuing, and well prepared and acted out scripts that seem to focus on specific terms;
2. The opening wide of an already ajar spiritual/material door or portal;
3. A legally binding negotiation for the soul of the one visited.

Again the Bible shows itself to be contemporary. Read the above in the context of the following Scripture and tell me that the same thing is not being repeated in many MIB encounters:

A direct quote from Scripture:

Direct examination of the witness: Now the serpent was more subtle than any beast of the field which the LORD God had made. And he said unto the woman, "Yea, hath God said, Ye shall not eat of every tree of the garden?"

Response by the witness: And the woman said unto the serpent, "We may eat of the fruit of the trees of the garden: But of the fruit of the tree which is in the midst of the garden, God hath said, Ye shall not eat of it, neither shall ye touch it, lest ye die."

Redress to that response: And the serpent said unto the woman, "Ye shall not surely die: For God doth know that in the day ye eat thereof, then your eyes shall be opened, and ye shall be as gods, knowing good and evil."

Entering in of the contract: "And when the woman saw that the tree was good for food, and that it was pleasant to the eyes, and a tree to be desired to make one wise, she took of the fruit thereof, and did eat, and gave also unto her husband with her; and he did eat." - Genesis 3:1-6 KJB

Having received the contract, Satan leaves. Note that he later tried the same thing when he tempted Jesus in the desert (St. Matthew 4:1-11 KJB. He left Jesus as well but without receiving any contract.)

Case Number 1 of a legal accounting involving a typical MIB visitation:

Direct Examination of the witness: Now the MIB were more subtle than any beast of the field which Satan had made. And the MIB said unto the woman, "Tell me, have you already spoken to anybody about what you saw?"

Response by the witness: And the woman said unto the MIB, "I saw a mysterious light in the sky and dutifully reported what I saw to the proper authorities."

Redress to that response: And the MIB said unto the woman, "If you know what's good for you, you won't speak about this anymore to anyone."

Entering in of the contract: The woman remains silent and succumbs to fear throughout the entire MIB intimidation process. She later responds to the veiled threats by altering her free-will behaviour in agreement with what she perceives to be her future state should she choose to ignore the warning. By altering her behavior physically, mentally and emotionally (Stockholm Syndrome) according to the terms of the perceived threat (opening of a spiritual/material door), she has just legally entered into a mutually binding agreement (negotiation for the soul of the one visited) with whoever sent these MIB as representatives (the fallen angels). The MIB leaves, having received the contract.

Case Number 2 of is a legal accounting involving a typical MIB visitation:

Direct Examination of the witness: Now the MIB were more subtle than any beast of the field which Satan had made. And the MIB said unto the woman, "I'm looking for so and so. Is he here?"

Response by the witness: And the woman said unto the MIB, "No he's not here right now but is expected back soon."

Redress to that response: And the MIB said unto the woman, "What would you say to a person if that person asked you to stop investigating these reports?"

Response by the witness: The woman responds by saying, "I'd tell that person to go to hell". At this point there can be no contract since the witness properly redressed the question despite the oppressive and dream-like psychological/paranormal pressure on her to feel intimidated or frightened.

Direct Examination of the witness: The MIB stares intently at the woman's pen lying on the desk.

Response by the witness: The woman notices his stare and offers the pen as a gift. She physically takes that pen and hands it over to him.

Entering in of the contract: The MIB receives the pen from her hand. At this point she has unwittingly entered into a mutually binding agreement as in Case Number 1 above.

The MIB leaves, cackling hysterically, having received the contract through another avenue of legal deception.

11.

"A short man in a black cape and top-hat"

A prime-mover in the Texas, USA office of the British-based Center for Fortean Zoology – one of the few, full-time groups that diligently searches the world for unknown animals, such as the Abominable Snowman, the Chupacabras and the Loch Ness Monster - Naomi West has a startling tale to relate that chronicles a series of events that occurred when she was a teenager, and which focuses upon two specific issues discussed in the *Introduction* to this very book: a hat-wearing MIB and a Mothman-type entity…

When I was 16, I lived in Parker City, Indiana. I always felt Indiana in general, and particularly Parker City, was very dark. I hated it there. Anyway, one night my friend Toby and I were at our friend Ralana's house. Ralana had just seen a mysterious light that she claimed occasionally appeared to her in her house. It had gone away just before we had arrived at Ralana's to visit. We all three thought it was probably an angel and we wanted to get it to come back. We decided that perhaps if we created a "holy atmosphere" by singing hymns and praying, we might get it to come back. So we shut ourselves in Ralana's parents' bedroom where the light had appeared to Ralana that evening, and we started singing, praying, etc. The room was entirely dark, having not even a window. We made sure that not a crack of light even showed beneath the door so that if the light did appear, we would know for sure it wasn't from a natural source.

After sitting in this pitch blackness having our impromptu church service, no light appeared, but I thought I saw something in front of me. It appeared to be black wings that extended up then back down as if in flight, almost in slow motion. Then I saw the head of the apparent black winged creature turn to the side. There was a long, snout-like nose on it. Because I didn't even believe what I was seeing - I mean, I truly thought my eyes were playing tricks on me - I dismissed it and said nothing about it. After all, when you are in a pitch black room, your eyes sometimes sort of create things, and this creature being black on black was so vague I just couldn't be sure. Before long, the three of us became bored of waiting for the light and we decided to leave.

On our way out the front door, it was either Ralana or Toby that said, somewhat tentatively, "Did anyone see a... black winged thing?"

The other two of us instantly said yes, we had. Then I remember specifically that Ralana said, "Did it have a beak-like snout on it?" We all agreed, realizing we had seen the very same creature. I can only assume that none of us had believed in what we were seeing at the time enough to mention it.

When I told my youth pastor the story later, he told me that we called up the "wrong" thing by trying to conjure anything at all. Of course, as kids, we hadn't considered our innocent attempts to invoke an angel "conjuring."

While reading your MIB book, I was reminded of a phenomenon that I want to know if you have heard about: I have a friend in WV named Debbie whose high-school boyfriend reported seeing a short man in a black cape and top-hat appear in his bedroom every night. Debbie is older than I am and this would have taken place in the mid-seventies. John, the boyfriend, was frightened of this figure, which would actually be close to his bed with each nightly appearance, and he took to sleeping with a baseball bat. My friend "went along with the crowd" and laughed at John when he told of this figure.

Not long afterward, John was in a car wreck that took his life after putting him in a coma for a long time. Debbie said that some time after John's death, she was driving one night and was horrified to see this very being John had described crossing the road right in front of her van. She took it as a sign that she needed to get her life straightened out - as she had been partying a lot - and believed that the figure somehow had been a foreshadowing of John's death. She told me this story back when I was about 16 and I never forgot it.

A few years ago, when I first came to Texas, I met a friend of my dad's named Jill - someone that had never met Debbie

- who told me that a friend of hers had seen a short, caped, figure in a top hat. Jill had never heard of this phenomenon before. One evening some time later, she was watching a TV interview in which someone reported seeing this very same entity. Jill was astonished to hear described the very thing her own friend had seen. I told Jill about Debbie and her boy-friend seeing the same thing.

I just wondered if you had heard of this particular "man in black" before. It doesn't sound like an actual MIB to me, but I'm convinced it's a real entity.

12.

"All I could hear
was static"

Claudia Cunningham was christened by long-time UFO researcher and author, Tim Beckley, as the "MIB Lady," due to her diligent and dedicated research into the phenomenon, as well as being someone who had her very own run in with one of the MIB in 2009, as I detailed in my book *The Real Men in Black*. In the late 1970s, Claudia experienced something else that many researchers of, and witnesses to, the Men in Black issue experience at least once in their lives: strange and unsettling telephone interference...

In the late '70s, I was married and my husband was a police officer who worked nights. Being alone and bored a lot I was heavily into reading of the paranormal through my massive little library - and I was then reading *Phone Calls from the Dead* by Scott Rogo. The gist was that when someone died they could call you and the book gave many instances of this happening. One famous person it happened to was the late actress Ida Lupino. Her father, London stage actor Stanley, supposedly called her from beyond the grave. It was eerie reading, believe me. One night I was in bed reading the book and I snapped on the AM radio on my night table, and the show was WGY's talk show and they were interviewing UFO abductee Betty Hill. She said she had a lot of phone interference after seeing the UFO with her husband Barney... static, that sort of thing. I was very nervous that night listening to it and imagining my phone would ring. Imagine my shock when it DID ring. This must have been around 9 PM at night...and all I could hear was static!! Like I say, I was heavily into reading anything about UFOs, Bermuda Triangle, etc. and I think my fear triggered the call. I mean, I think fear attracts these entities and they were having, as John Lennon would say, "a larf" on yours truly.

Second incident...I was a gal who liked to go out on weekends as anyone would in their early 20s. I was dating Denny Cunningham, who I would later marry. Denny worked at the Postal Service before getting on the Albany, NY Police department and he worked nights. I would drive in from my parents' home in Glenmont to Albany and meet him, just usually for a chat and to watch Johnny Carson's Tonight Show together at his parents' home.

On Fridays and Saturdays my parents would go out to meet another couple for dinner and drinks and not return until sometimes 2-3 AM. Now, when you leave Albany en-route to my house, you go down what used to be a very rural road (now it's all built up, but in the late 60s it was very desolate.) You had to pass a huge Catholic cemetery and when you pulled in my driveway there was and is a field with high weeds. I always imagined that someone could be waiting for me and do something awful. I've always had a very vivid imagination!

I did have an incident where a man followed me home one night and pulled a pen knife out of his pocket after I pulled in the driveway. He was trying to run me off the road… it was terrifying. This happened after the incident I will now tell you about. But to return to the subject at hand, between the fear of breaking down in front of the cemetery and the field next to the house, I was always very nervous.

I ran into the house, dreading the fact that it would be dark and I'd be alone. No one was home but "us chickens" as my grandmother used to say. I immediately turned on a light on the mantel and retired to my bedroom, heart beating heavily, to await my parents' return. I no sooner got to my bedroom than my brand new pink rotary phone with a PRIVATE UNLISTED number I had just gotten, (*free* as it happens, compliments of my employer, NY Telephone Co.) rung! Denny never called me that late. He never called to see if I made it home or anything. Three people had the number - Dennis, his sister and my friend, Ann. I had just gotten the phone. No one had my number, OK?

A man with a guttural and threatening voice said very emphatically, "Claudia? I see you just got home. Do you know KNOW what I'm going to do with you? I'm coming over now"…and hung up!!!!!!! I thought I would absolutely die on the spot. Just think, now…a brand new phone with a brand new number... no one had it. If a neighbor saw me pull in, they wouldn't have my phone number to call me, so it was no neighbor. I heard a car pull in the driveway as I was planning to run out through the cellar through the cellar door to escape...and it was my parents! Thank the Good Lord.

I never found out who it was, nor do I want to know. I was involved in my studying UFOs, etc. and I was always very nervous and upset around that time to begin with. As many young girls know, and especially in that time, it was very important to get married. Denny was kind of balking, and I was miserable. Besides, I hated my job...so I was nervous all the time and emotional. Again, my private fears and my interest in strange subjects must have pulled some entity to me just to frighten me. Well, whoever it was succeeded beyond their wildest dreams.

Third incident: Denny's sister, Dorothy Jeffers, was taking care of a neighbor who had cancer, an older lady. Her family was kind of broken up and the kids never really had much of an interest in her, so Dottie would stop by and bring her groceries, call her to check on her, etc. The lady passed on...I think her name was Margaret or Minnie.

One night about two weeks after she passed away, Dottie had just finished doing the nightly dishes after dinner when the phone ring. There was much crackling on the line and static, then a faint tiny voice - unmistakably the old lady's - said, "Dottie? Thank you for taking care of me"...and the line went dead. She said it was absolutely, positively the lady's voice. Me? I think it could have been a demonic entity posing as the neighbor. At any rate, it happened, it was real…so we'll put it down to being a very great mystery.

13.

"Men in Black are neither hallucinations nor hoaxes"

Born on March 3, 1952, Robert A. Goerman is a native of New Kensington, Pennsylvania. As an investigative scholar of unknown and unexplained phenomena, he has been fortunate enough to have his writings featured in national magazines and serve as source material for many books and popular television shows such as *Unsolved Mysteries, The Unexplained, History's Mysteries, Animal X, MonsterQuest,* and *Dark Matters: Twisted But True.* Founded in June of 2012, his Nonhuman Research Agency explores encounters with mysterious strangers, beings, and creatures and studies interspecific relationships. Robert offers his very own insights into the MIB mystery, based upon his firsthand investigations of a very weird case from the 1960s that is steeped in menace of the black-colored kind. It is a case that has led Robert to some thought-provoking theories concerning the nature and actions of the MIB, too…

One bizarre Pennsylvania case (that I personally investigated) began on the night of January 20, 1967, when Mrs. Walter

Kushner and her two daughters, Susan (17) and Tanya (14) and a close friend of the girls, Marianne Williamson (16), witnessed a brilliant UFO drop below the cloud cover and maneuver at high speed while the four were returning to the Kushner's Pittsfield residence. Hours later, as the three girls enjoyed a ritual teenage slumber party, they spotted a peculiar light shimmering through the closed curtains of Susan's bedroom.

Without warning, the drapes parted of their own volition and a small triangular object hovering a few feet from the house began beaming brilliant light into the bedroom. When the triangle moved to another window, the curtains repeated their opening act and the intensity of light emanating from the object increased. At this point, the girls became quite frightened and decided to retreat. "It" had different ideas.

All three girls found themselves unable to move or cry out. Sheer terror escalated to fervent prayers for help. After what seemed like an eternity, the siege ended. Although their freedom of movement was restored, a weird dizzy sensation haunted the girls for an hour. The girls awoke Mrs. Kushner and tearfully described the party crasher and their fear that "it" might return. Mother eventually got the trio settled down and after much discussion decided that it would be for the best if everyone simply forgot an incident that nobody would believe anyway. All agreed.

Things were back to normal when shortly after the dinner hour on Saturday, exactly one week following the horrific pajama party, two men arrived at the Kushner household. They identified themselves as military investigators and flashed what appeared to be United States Air Force identification. Both men wore tan trench-coats that they kept buttoned from knee to collar. The taller of the two, who, according to the family's testimony, did all the talking, was described as having blond hair, green eyes, and was thin and deeply tanned. The other gentleman was heavyset with dark hair, piercing blue eyes and was also deeply tanned.

Mrs. Kushner explained that both men wanted every shred of information regarding the UFO that the girls claimed had intimidated them. Neither parent can explain to this day why they allowed their children to be so intensely grilled by these "government agents." These characters moved about the house with apparently total knowledge of the whereabouts of rooms, furniture, objects, et cetera. When asked how the Air Force learned of the UFO sightings, the taller one responded with, "We know a lot of things, a lot of things."

Although compelled to accept the situation, the family felt that something seemed off-center, something that, for whatever reason, they couldn't quite put their finger on until after the officers departed. Sue noted that their clothes looked as if they had purchased them in a clothing store ten minutes before and even the bottom of their shoes seemed un-walked on in appearance. The cigarette pack held by the taller one was unopened (and stayed that way) and even his wallet was brand new.

While the taller of the two showed his captive audience a loose-leaf notebook with professionally printed schematic diagrams and photos of both the exterior and interior views of various types of UFO-type craft, Sue watched the shorter officer secretly write in an elongated notebook not unlike those used by stenographers. Catching him off guard, she was amazed to see him writing strange symbols in vertical columns, starting from the left, going down one column, up the next, down the third, up the fourth, et cetera. Being accustomed to standard shorthand, Sue had no idea of the graphic's origin.

Meanwhile, the talkative officer continued to mystify his audience, telling them that UFOs were nothing more than secret U. S. experimental devices which have never harmed persons or property and that public disclosure of seeing one up close could result in criminal prosecution.

When Tanya asked how the family could get in touch with them should there be another sighting, the officer replied, "I can find you anywhere, any time."

When these military men finally left, they backed their vehicle out onto the roadway, extinguished the headlights and zoomed off into the night. It is against Pennsylvania commonwealth traffic laws, and all common sense and safety, to drive after sunset without suitable lighting. These gentlemen probably had no connection with the United States Air Force.

Men in Black are neither hallucinations nor hoaxes. But what do these visitations represent? Role-playing covert government operatives? Nonhumans acting human? Maybe a little of both. Maybe something beyond our comprehension. Odd appearance and bizarre behavior does not certify the existence of nonhumans among us. However, dissolving coins and cars raise interesting questions. Our failure to understand these events in no way negates their validity.

These visitations represent entity contact at its most accessible in that entire families have endured grueling visits by these mystery men and many witnesses are harassed more than once. These visitations represent entity contact at its most elusive. Parents wonder why they allowed their children to be so intensely grilled by these strangers. Victims speak of being unable to think or react normally until after the mysterious visitors leave. To some, this suggests altered states of consciousness or subliminal hypnotic techniques.

What if the MIB visit you? Will you be witty and clever and insist they pose for a snapshot? Or will you be a deer in headlights and spend your tomorrows wondering why?

14.

"He was staring right into my soul"

Neil Arnold hails from the centuries-old and folklore-filled county of Kent, England, and is the author of many acclaimed titles of a mysterious and supernatural nature, including *Monster! The A-Z to Zooform Phenomena; Mystery Animals of the British Isles: Kent; Shadows in the Sky; and Paranormal London*. Of his personal and surreal exposure to the Men in Black phenomenon, Neil relates two stories of bizarre proportions...

During the early '90s I was with two mates out walking at night, and I'd just got the reissues of *The Unexplained* magazine - and we saw a strange, hanging, dull yellow light in the sky which at first we took to be a firework about to explode. It was late October. The light eventually came over us, at quite a height and the light vanished (I believe because it was on top of the object). But the underside revealed a circle of lights and we watched in amazement as this thing silently glided over the houses out of sight. I recall a chap walking his dog that also looked up at it and everything was very quiet. Although

I don't recall it, when I spoke to one of the guys many years later (I lost touch with him shortly afterwards), he stated quite categorically that we lost about an hour in time.

This is not something I've ever taken seriously. Anyway, a month or so later, I began writing a lot about MIB's and UFOs, and the same two friends visited London to buy records. It was early afternoon and we were sat in the MacDonald's in Leicester Square. I was facing the door, one of my mates faced me with his back to the door, and my other mate sat side on. I recall looking up over my mate's shoulder (the mate who was facing me) and there was a guy sitting there.

He was about ten-feet away, staring, what I felt was, right into my soul. He was about 60-70 years of age, he had grey hair slicked back, wide, unblinking eyes. He wore a black suit, white shirt and a dark tie. Strangely, he had no food on the table, no newspaper and he just sat staring at me.

I went to mention it to my friend who was facing me and my mate just shuddered and said, "I know!" He said he could sense this guy. We actually got up and left straight away...very odd.

I also have a relative who in the '80s saw a UFO and went to the local phone box to report it to the newspaper. As soon as he entered the phone box a man appeared beside it and was staring in rather menacingly. My relative thought the man wanted to use the phone and so he motioned he wouldn't be long, but the man still stared.

The man wore a dark suit. My relative came off the phone

and said to the man: "You can use it now." But he just stood there. My relative told the newspaper that he would go to their offices to tell them of the sighting, but as soon as he got on the bus he got a shocking headache. He thought he was going to pass out but persisted, but when he got to the office no-one working there knew what he was on about and they all said they hadn't received a call from him.

15.

"I was to be visited by these strange men in the dead of night"

Trevor Owen, a citizen of the United Kingdom, relates a story that dates back to his pre-teen years of the late-1970s, and which is filled with trauma, nightmares and a certain group of characters in dark clothing...

When I was a boy, I had some very strange encounters with what I can only refer to as the MIB. I think first I should start with the incident that I believe brought them to me, for this I have to go back to the year 1977.

I was 12 years old and I lived in the countryside; a friend had asked me to do his early morning paper round whilst he was on holiday for a week. You had to be 13 years old to do an early morning paper round, but as there was no-one else to do it in the quiet village, the distributors allowed me.

One of those mornings I was cycling down Bailes Lane, a dead end road with common land at the end. It went for miles toward the nearest town Guildford and had a couple of farms that were accessible by tracks from the end of the lane onto the common land. As I was cycling past the fields on the way to the end, I felt something on my shoulder. I turned to look and there looking straight at me was a bird, a bird of prey no less, it looked like a Buzzard. I had the feeling that it was saying "hello" to me. I said hello back in my mind and it then took off and flew away.

As I turned a corner and pedaled up a slight incline towards the end of the lane, ahead and to the right under the dark cloud cover was a bright light. It was elliptical in shape and had very defined edges despite the light emanating from it being extremely bright, brighter than any normal light. It was completely silent, and moving in a slow South Easterly direction towards Guildford. The idea of space and its inhabitants was of interest to me; I watched *Dr. Who* and *UFO* and *Space 1999* with glee and excitement. I would imagine a spaceship coming down and the jolly spacemen inviting me aboard to see the ship and maybe even take me for a trip.

But on seeing this ship of light in front of me, I stopped pedaling and became motionless. In fact I found that I was extremely scared and was now unable to move any of my limbs. I wanted to turn around and cycle home as fast as possible to get away, but I was frozen, like a rabbit caught in the headlights of a car.

The ship slowly passed across in front of me, silently. It was perhaps 50 to 100 foot across, I couldn't be sure as I was not able to judge the distance, maybe bigger? It was just under cloud height but was perhaps 10cm at arm's length and about 50 to 60 degrees from the horizon (at a guess). My head and eyes moved with the craft as it went across the horizon; it was involuntary movement as the only thing I really wanted to move was my legs in furious pedaling!

All the time as I could see the craft, in my head I was saying a mantra: "Don't come near me, don't come near me, don't come near me; go away, go away, go away."

Over and over again I said this in my head as the ship passed silently in front me. Now it was off to the left of me and the clouds had a few breaks in them; the craft went behind a cloud, came out, went behind another cloud, came out, went behind another cloud…this time it didn't come out. After a few seconds when I was sure that it had gone and didn't return, full use of my limbs became restored and I was able to cycle back home in a rush.

After this encounter, but I couldn't say how long, because I did not connect the two episodes until many years later you must understand.

I was to be visited by these strange men in the dead of night, not when I was awake in my room, but when I was asleep. They would not present themselves physically in my room (I don't think?), but rather they would come into my dreams. I was not aware of their meaning for many years until I learned of the men in black and finally remembered these boyhood nightmares.

What would happen is I would dream of these two men; they were featureless, as in they had no faces that I could remember, and they were dressed as business men (as I thought of them at the time), black trousers and jackets and ties, white shirts and black hats. They would always be after me and I would always be running away from them. The feeling they gave was not just one of pursuit, but it also had a sexual nature to it. I always felt that they were chasing me and were after my butt, as I remember having a strange tingling sensation in that area.

I was quite confused about these dreams and obviously wondered what they meant. I did wonder for a while if it meant I was becoming homosexual, which was a really scary thought to me, but that did not turn out to be the case. So I put it down to just one of those things you go through when growing up, perhaps just strange feelings that are a part of adjusting to becoming an adult?

The really puzzling thing though is why would the men in black chase someone in their dreams, especially when the victim does not even know of the men in black? And indeed they never caught and told me exactly why they were chasing me, or that I should never speak of my close encounter, not that I remember anyway. The feeling of them being after my butt could be the most effective way of scaring a young boy, or even perhaps a memory of my possible abduction (remember the bird of prey, birds sometimes being remembered instead of aliens) where part of it could have been an internal examination going in through the anus?

Because of the sexual nature of my feelings in these dreams, I was never going to tell anyone about them, and only recently have dared to come forward with such a bizarre and unsettling story. However, it does show that some of these entities cannot just be physical, but are also of a psychic (projecting their thoughts and presence into the mind of the experience), ethereal or other dimensional nature, in my opinion.

I have no idea exactly who they are, and although they purport to scare people into silence, the one thing they do achieve, is to confirm to the experiencer that what they saw was not an imagination but something real and worth scaring you into silence over! A confirmation of sorts, so could it be that the owners of these crafts are giving a nod to say, yep we were there! Are they responsible for the follow up visits?

One thing I "feel" is certain: my witnessing or possible abduction was no accident; they at least wanted me to remember seeing the craft. I have one more adage to this story. Many years later, less than ten years ago now, I had another dream, not of the MIB but of me being in a field, and coming towards me was an attractive lady. She had short blonde hair and was really smiling widely, she looked so beautiful, and I mean not as she was attractive, but another sort of beauty, an inner one that seemed to come across. I remember I was looking up at her, so I must have been small (young) and she outstretched her hands towards me, as if to pick me up or hug me or something. This is the part I remember vividly, because there was something strange about her hands: she had six fingers! This is where the dream ended. But it had a certain quality to it.

I am of the opinion that it could be a surfacing memory

about when I was a boy cycling past that field, when a bird landed on my shoulder. Is that where I was meeting with the occupants of that craft I saw after? Was there missing time on that paper round? I'm not 100 percent sure, but when I cycled home without even finishing the paper route, and wouldn't go out again, they asked where I had been and wouldn't believe my story about the UFO. Perhaps I will never remember everything, but I hope one day I get the answers I search for.

16.

"This shadow wore a black fedora"

Patricia tells us of her trauma-filled experience with a shadowy, nightmarish, fedora-wearing fiend…

I just finished reading your book, "The Real Men In Back." I was particularly interested in Part II: The Theories. I am 62 years old, from a town near the Mississippi River across from St. Louis. I grew up in the country, next to a lake. This is pertinent because I do believe that water can be a conduit for paranormal phenomena. And, I am also a Pisces.

I include my age because what happened to me was before any kind of media frenzy about UFOs, or abduction stories were made popular by books or movies. I am a former art teacher and artist, extremely creative, was the quintessential flower child in the 60s, all of which works against one as far as credibility is concerned. It began when I was quite young. I had night terrors every night. Afraid to sleep alone (my bedroom was the closest to the lake), I ended up in my parents bed up until I was almost 16 years old.

I always imagined something was in my room.

What happened one night, shook me to the core, for years.

I was around 16 (already having periods) when, as I began dozing off, I saw a thin black shadow with a large head peek around my door looking at me. I didn't feel right, couldn't focus or move and was basically paralyzed while the "shadow" mounted me, and what I guess was, having sex. Remember, 16 year old girls then were far more naive than today. I fell into a very deep sleep.

I was troubled for weeks and then when time for my period came around, it didn't. I was terrified, and couldn't figure out what had happened to me, because I wasn't sexually active. My period began the following month. Now, a person might say that nerves alone could interfere with female cycles, BUT, throughout my entire "female" life, I had only skipped 3 periods. Once, when I was very ill and hospitalized while living in Venezuela, secondly, when pregnant with my son... and thirdly, this incident with the black shadow person. I put it out of my mind until many, many years later when the alien abduction/impregnation theories became popular. I am not saying this was my case.

Now, for my MIB stories. About 5 or 6 years later while finishing up my art degree, I shared a house with another art student who, incidentally, was very psychic. We had some terrifying events take place in a small, old basement-less wood framed house, where we spent our senior year. I always heard my named being called out, the telephone would ring at strange hours of the night with no one on the other end... and interestingly enough, about 30 seconds after the phone would ring, our animals, in opposite ends of the house (2 birds and a cat) would flap violently in the cage and the cat would go shrieking around my roommate's studio. It always took us about five minutes to quiet them down.

Then one night, I was visited by another shadow person. This shadow wore a black fedora and either a bulky black coat or a cape. I saw only its silhouette. I was pinned down with my arms over my head in a brain fog. I felt if I didn't scream out, I would be taken. He just stood at the foot of my bed. I finally bolted up and at that same moment the animals began their flapping and shrieking.

For the rest of the semester, I slept in my roommate's studio and only went into my room for clothing. Just two years ago, my husband and I were driving back from Austin and drove through my old college town. We stopped by my senior house and I spoke to the current owner. He said he had never had any kind of paranormal event there, and was surprised when I was so adamant about my experiences.

The third and last shadow person came to me when I was around 35. I used to travel a lot and took a trip to Paris by myself. The first night I once again found myself with my arms pinned back, up over my head in a brain fog. The shadow man was the same as the one before, but bigger. After a "struggle," I awakened myself, terrified, and didn't sleep the rest of the night. I was afraid of the huge, long

Parisian windows in the room, thinking that something had come into my room that way. It was a difficult trip after that, because I did not sleep well.

I read your Part II: The Theories, while thinking of my experiences. I wonder if all of the black shadow men, in fedoras and black suits or capes that people around the world see, are actually MIBs. Throughout my adult life, I have had very vivid dreams of UFOs. The last, most vivid in sepia tones, was just last week.

I just wish that 40 years ago, I had books like yours to read. Keep them coming...

17.

"It was like something out of The Exorcist"

Kathy Kasten, who passed away in August 2012 at the age of 72, was a frequent and feisty contributor to the now-defunct online discussion group, *UFO Updates*. She also wrote for *Paranoia* – which had a near-twenty-year run on the newsstands in magazine format. In April 2010, however, the publication received a radical overhaul and, today, is available as a series of on-going trade paperbacks.

Very appropriately, Kathy's own experiences of the MIB variety were steeped in deep and wretched paranoia. Her curious stories, told to me only a few months before she died, go like this...

So many highly strange events have happened in my life. Sometimes I forget some of them. Briefly, I returned from a vacation to find that the company I worked for had hired someone named Linda. The company, Natelson, Levander, & Whitney, were consultants to commercial and government clients. They surveyed, dug into information, etc., about parcels of land the client was interested in and produced reports.

Linda sat at the front reception area with Carolina. My desk was in the middle of the suite of offices. Linda asked me out to lunch to tell me she had been hired to be office manager. I thought that was very odd that she was providing this information, and wondered if it was true.

The next lunch invite, Linda went right to the point. She played it a little on the cagey side, suggesting we walk and talk. It was then she related to me her abduction experiences - or what she thought were abductions by ETs. She had read Whitley Strieber's book, *Communion*. At the time, I knew nothing about abductions, Strieber or his book. Whatever bait she was tossing out, I didn't bite. It was very soon after that I was never invited to lunch with Linda. Plus, she gave her notice she was leaving to return to care for a family member. I believe she had claimed to be an RN.

Anyway, she left. Carolina and I were now carrying the workload. I was forever making trips to the front desk to interact with Carolina. During one of my forays, as I was bending down talking to Carolina, I looked up and there was a very short, almost bald man of indiscriminate age standing on the other side of the reception area counter. The counter rose to just a little under my breastbone. The guy was really short and wore a plaid shirt that did not match in anyway shape or form the plaid of his pants. Very white and pasty looking. He never took his eyes off me the entire time he stood in front of us.

I rose up and stood facing him, affecting my street attitude style. As if to say, "Come on, give it to me and see what happens." I don't remember what he said because I was focused on the fact the smile on his face did not match what he was saying.

I seem to remember Carolina moving her chair closer to me while still sitting down. I didn't pick up any creepy feelings. I was just irritated with the interruption of my work. He left. As I remember it, he had whisked in and whisked out. Not really disappearing. But, he moved very fast. That wasn't the end of this guy.

The building where the office was located was on the SW corner of Wilshire and Gayley in LA. When I left the office that evening, I walked south on Gayley. As I walked I noticed the Men in Plaid (MIP) across the street pacing me. Not behind me, but ahead of me. I slowed down. He slowed down.

I think I said something like: "What has this guy got: eyes in the back of his head?" At which point, his head turned to face me while his body kept facing forward walking at our shared pace. It was like something out of *The Exorcist*. It was not a normal head swivel. That wasn't the end of it.

The next day, I shared with Carolina what had happened and reminded her of this guy coming to our offices. She claimed that we never had any visitors that previous afternoon. I kept insisting we had. She insisted that we hadn't. End of that episode.

It was most assuredly not the end of Kathy's experiences with enigmatic, unsettling characters, however. She continued to me as follows, in relation to the ever-controversial Roswell affair of July 1947, and the man who kick-started the furor: rancher William Ware "Mack" Brazel...

While traveling with two members of my field team in and around Corona, New Mexico, I had wanted to have a site verified by one of the team members. We had been driving NW on Pine Lodge Road - the same one Brazel had used to drive into Roswell. I was driving a late model Cadillac with all the bells and whistles. It wasn't safe to travel faster than about 5 or 10 miles an hour. Finally, I found the ranch I had seen once before. My lawyer had told me not to climb any fences that posted "*No Trespassing!*" We parked when I spotted what I was looking for - a white domed shaped building. I wanted Richard to see it. Greg refused to get out of the car. Richard refused to climb the fence with me, but he could see the white domed building I had talked about.

One of the peculiar things about this building was that on the local map I was looking at, that exact crinkle in the road was called "Dulce." Hah! We were hot and thirsty and decided to move on. Further up the road, we came upon a gorge that opened into a valley. Sitting in the middle of nowhere must have been the oldest bar in New Mexico. It was called the *White Oak Saloon*. It had real atmosphere up the wazoo.

I recommend it if you ever find yourself on the Pine Lodge Road. It turned out the owner had married a woman from Traverse City, MI. My team member, Richard, just happened to know her from high school days. She was not around during our visit, but there was plenty of talk about: all the gold to be found in the area. I was leaning over the bar counter staring at the nuggets of gold under glass.

Suddenly, I turned to watch a very skinny, pasty looking, arms hanging to his knees, no hair sticking out from under what seemed like a 20 to 30 gallon white/ivory colored cowboy hat. Once again, there was the plaid shirt. This time with black pants. I think it was the high heel cowboy boots that hardened my opinion of "this guy is ridiculous."

He took a seat next to the open door. Nobody acknowledged him. He acknowledged nobody in the saloon. I think I remember two people behind the bar, two guys sitting at a table, Greg sitting at a table, Richard and me at the bar. The guy just sat there staring at me. He was boring me and I turned my attention to the conversation I was part of at the bar. So I don't remember him leaving. But, he did leave without acknowledgement from anybody in the bar. Now, you and I know some of the informal rites of drinking in a local bar. Usually, somebody will say goodbye, such as the remaining people in the bar. We left to go back on the road to Corona. For sometime after that, none of my team remembered the strange cowboy who stepped into the saloon, took a seat by the open door, said nothing, contributed nothing, and then left.

It wasn't until just recently that Richard brought up that he remembered the White Oak Saloon and the strange cowboy.

There you have it: my MIP – Men in Plaid - stories. You want strange and stranger.

And there is still more from Kathy, too; three accounts which Kathy shared with me not long before she passed away:

A trip to Cambridge, England: This trip had been planned for at least six months prior to making it; visa arrangements had to be made; contact and plans made with the sponsoring institution – UCLA [University of California, Los Angeles]. Therefore, an agency with the means and ways to find out when and where I was going had plenty of time to assign someone to follow me. On the flight to England, I felt someone staring at the back of my aisle seat. I turned to see a man four rows back from me, also on an aisle seat, quickly avert his eyes.

I thought it odd behavior, but discounted it as just a curious observer; although, the "stare" seemed very intense. I was at Cambridge for a three week summer course. On the return flight? Sure enough, exactly four rows behind me, once again in an aisle seat, was the same man dressed in the same suit. Needless to say, I stared back for more time than is considered polite. The entire time the man's eyes stayed averted. Not the normal response when someone is staring at you.

I had to return my suitcases to the storage facility in Santa Monica, California. After depositing the luggage in my storage room, the manager of the facility – during the elevator ride back down to the bottom floor – remarked that there was something odd going on in the facility parking lot. And, I might want to be careful when I went back to my vehicle.

The elevator opened on the loading dock and sitting in the parking lot were only two vehicles. One of them was mine and the other a late model Mercedes-Benz. A silver white-haired guy, dressed in white shirt and pants – shirt opened almost to the waist wearing a long gold chain with large medallion - was getting back into his vehicle. He had parked his vehicle exactly next to my driver's door at a slight angle to hide any movement between his vehicle and mine. There was plenty of room in the large parking lot and yet this guy had decided to park basically too close to my vehicle.

The manager remarked to me, as I started to move out of the elevator onto the dock platform, that the guy had not come into the facility. She told me that she had watched him through her office window until the phone rang. She held me back until he pulled out of the parking lot. His vehicle was finely tuned and made next to no sound as it backed up and drove out of the lot. I got into my vehicle and noticed that the briefcase I had carried with me to and from England was missing. It had been sitting on the passenger seat of my vehicle when I got out. At that time, there had been no other vehicle in the lot.

After discovering the briefcase was missing, I thought

to myself that I hoped whoever wanted the briefcase enjoyed the course required paper I had written on archeo-astronomy, along with a poem written to commemorate a visit to West Kennet megalithic burial site. At the time of this incident, I was still on a project with my friend from Mexico who worked as a consultant for the Mexican government agency involved in oil and thought about his tales of missing briefcases. However, our joint project was focused on archaeology, not oil. I had to wonder if someone thought I was acting as a courier for my friend.

Stealth Van Visit – Los Angeles, West Side.

Some 14 or 15 years after the event where my briefcase was removed from my vehicle, the archaeology project was finished and I moved on to researching mind control technology. I was writing articles for a magazine on this subject and communicating with targets of electronic mind control through on-line chat rooms. I knew about ECHELON (a system where electronic messages are intercepted by receiving stations that sift through non-military domestic and business communications including e-mail, telephone, fax networks) and NSA monitoring and searching for communications containing specific words.

There is no doubt in my mind that because of the above monitoring there was a real possibility of lurkers (people who monitor chat groups without letting their presence be known) and that some agency was aware of my research. The knowledge of this electronic technology to control and monitor targets is something that people in power would rather the general public didn't know about. I had culled information from technical papers, books in UCLA's Biomed Library that had been read by the UCLA faculty involved in MKUltra (a U.S. government project that researched methods of mind control) and research documents from around the world. The outcome of this research was that I was able to link various aspects of the technology to provide a cohesive picture of how the technology affected humans.

During this time, there had been attempts to invade my work place by person's unknown and create a hostile environment. One of the perpetrators had attempted to involve the staff working in office in our section of the basement – in the UCLA Department of Pathology, Section of Cytology – by calling a person in each office to tell them I was dangerous and they should be careful of me. The phone calls were done within minutes of each other. It caused quite a flurry of activity as my coworkers came to my office to tell me what was happening. But, everybody was too busy with the work of the department to take the guy seriously. Good thing my coworkers were intelligent enough to ask for specific examples of why I needed to be watched and asked the name of the caller. The caller would hurriedly hang up without answering their questions.

Finally, when that wasn't working, the guy called me

directly stating that he knew where my office was located and he was coming after me; knew how to garrote a human being because of his training in the military; had associations with the FBI. I asked for his name. The guy hung up. But almost immediately I started receiving threatening e-mails making the same claims. I downloaded the e-mails and called the FBI to tell them somebody called me impersonating an FBI agent. During the phone call, the FBI agent arranged that we meet as soon as possible. The FBI office was located in the Federal Building on Wilshire Boulevard, blocks from UCLA. After reading the e-mails and listening to my report, the two agents took the threat seriously and we setup a wire trap. But, the guy never called again.

The next incident happened not too long after the threatening calls. A young woman forced her way into the Frozen Section area of the department (located next to the Operating Room) by using my name and providing some story about needing to see me. My coworkers in the Frozen Section knew me and wanted to help the distressed woman. Everybody knew where my office was. It was on the same basement level as the Frozen Section area of the department.

Standing in the doorway of my office, she threatened to hurt me if I did not help her. She was rudely interrupting a conference with one of the doctors I worked for. We were discussing a work related matter. When the doctor heard the tone in the woman's voice, the doctor quickly excused himself and left my office. What help the young woman thought

I could provide wasn't made very clear. She made stabbing movements into the air with a finger, jerking her body as she moved closer to my desk. The desk separated us. Her eyes were glazed over; she appeared to be on drugs.

I picked up the phone and started to dial Security; telling her what I was doing. Nothing she was saying made any sense. One of my coworkers – who worked in the lab across from my office – heard the loud conversation and silently moved in behind the woman. My hall mate had played football in high school. The woman must have felt him standing behind her, quickly turned around, looked at him and decided to leave.

After these strange incidents, I was on "high alert." It was my habit to have a late night cigar smoke in my vehicle to relax; ear buds plugged into the radio listening to music. Usually, I sat in the driver's seat. You should know that my vehicle at the time was a very large truck with very large outside rearview mirrors. Every once in a while, I would check traffic through the rearview mirror. During one of those checks, what appeared in my mirror seemed to be a vehicle from a science fiction movie. It had an array of antennas across the top of the cab section; there wasn't a curved surface on the thing; it was painted the blackest color one can imagine.

I couldn't see it unless it was directly under a street light. Most astonishing to me was that it pulled up and stopped exactly so that our windows were even with each other. My window was already open to let out the cigar smoke. Their window lowered without a sound. There was a flash of light.

My subconscious reaction was to take a big draw off the cigar and blow it at them. Another flash meant someone had captured me on film blowing a puff of smoke. Their window went back up and the vehicle moved forward.

My immediate reaction was to toss down the cigar in the street, jump out of my vehicle, grabbing the keys, and chase after the futuristic van. It had turned just ahead of me into a long street containing old growth trees whose branches met in the middle of the street. There wasn't much light from the few streetlights. The van must have pulled up under one of those trees and disappeared into the darkness because it didn't seem to be anywhere in sight. I decided I would have been pushing my luck to walk up to the van and basically challenge their right to photograph me. So, I let it go.

The next day, I called an "insider" friend and described the vehicle to him. I was told that the stealth van was kept at El Toro Air Base and only operated under the command of the President of the U.S. Clinton was president at the time of the above described incident. I said over the phone to my friend that I hoped Clinton enjoyed the photo. As I remember it, the tune through the ear buds – while being under close surveillance – was the mellow tones of the alto saxophone of John Coltrane playing *The Night Has a Thousand Eyes*. I have always thought of that this as a very inside joke known only to myself.

Summation: There was no way to tell what the two people in the stealth van were wearing. We could assume they were dressed in some type of flight suit of very black material with Secret Service patches on the shoulder and/or sleeve. Or, some type of clothing that made them appear to disappear into the interior of the van cab.

My final story for you happened one morning as I left for work. The following event happened almost two or three years after the stealth van event. It was garbage collection day in West Los Angeles and I needed to dump some trash in the curbside container located in the alley which connected only a few feet from the dead-end street. My back was to the street for what must have been approximately 1 second. I didn't even hear the late model Mercedes-Benz vehicle pull up across from me. We were separated by a grass strip of the old Santa Monica street car tracks that ran from Century City to Santa Monica.

Parts of the tracks still remain here and there, and the strip of land was an oasis in a heavily developed part of Los Angeles. Again here was the same model as the storage facility agent, silver or white haired, white shirt and black pants, but this time the shirt was buttoned up all the way to the chin button. No gold medallion, but this guy was holding a very large cigar and waving it around so that I could see it while he was standing near the front of the hood, keeping the vehicle between us. He was making it obvious the show he was putting on was for my benefit. When he was sure I saw him, he got into the vehicle, but kept the cigar in the air so that I could see it over the top of the vehicle. He drove off. Once again, I noticed there was no sound from the engine.

Summation: all three vehicles involved in the surveillance were so finely tuned that there was next to no engine noise, or any of the usual noise associated with motor vehicles. (Don't we all wish we could have the same mechanic working on our vehicles.) Who were these guys? Who assigned them to monitor me so overtly? The stealth van incident is obvious – the Secret Service was ordered by someone on the White House staff. Exactly who is unknown. The new improved men-in-black-and-white? Unknown, but they certainly drive very nice expensive cars.

There you have it. My contribution to true stories of being followed. These are just a couple out of the many. I only wanted to provide a couple of examples showing that anybody can and will be monitored.

18.

"Beings that don't quite fit the mold"

Micah Hanks is a writer and radio personality. He is a frequent traveler, lecturer, and researcher of historic mysteries, myth and culture, political topics, anthropology, and unexplained aerial phenomenon. He is author of four books, with his latest, *The Ghost Rockets,* dealing with unexplained missile incidents from the 1940s to the present day. His websites are micahhanks.com and gralienreport.com, where podcasts, books, and articles can be found...

The Night Walkers: Myth, Evil, and the Men in Black
– By Micah Hanks

If ever there were one lingering haunter in the darkness, chosen perhaps to represent the collective fears and paranoia of the self-ascribed UFO believer today, few would object to that most-feared among the secretive spooks, the Man in Black, being pinned with such a title.

Particularly in America, the MIB has remained a haunting fixture within our culture; a staple, of sorts, representing the mask of secrecy that underlies the study of strange objects seen in our skies. This, placing conspiracies of the otherworldly variety aside for the moment, may be in large part due to the kind of stoic concern our government agencies—namely the U.S. Air Force—had shown with regard to the mounting UFO problem in the years immediately following the Second World War.

America was thrust into a new technological era, where the fruits of the World War II's labors had bestowed the eventual victors with tremendous new strength, as well as the lingering threat of mutual destruction between global superpowers. There was, at times, a solemn attitude our government had taken with regard to the potential for new technologies instigating another international conflict; and hence, the motivations of keeping secret projects away from public view, or even resorting to vague measures of threat and intimidation for purposes of suppressing those who might occasionally see something they shouldn't have, become all too apparent in retrospect.

The curious and unsettling visitations by men dressed in black plainclothes suits could, for some, be easily legitimized by arguing that government agents (and ones that were per-haps even more paranoid than the civilians they visited) were behind the entire MIB mess. And yet, of the ongoing phe-nomenon, so much more could indeed be said, taking into consideration the wealth of stories shared by those claiming to have had the experience themselves. The more otherworldly aspects of the MIB presence often include the appearance of beings that, while resembling humans like you or I, don't quite fit the mold, so to speak. Beings that have variously been described as "robotic," or even "ghostly" with pallid discolored skin, donning opaque and darkened eyewear, and sometimes long-brimmed hats to further obscure their features.

We could not assert that there is truly any characteristic that clearly betrays the *inhumanity* of such individuals, if they do exist. However, the sensations they tend to evoke with their isolated and unwanted appearances often convey an unsettling air; at times the MIB experience is so inescapably strange—or *absurd*—that it seems to bear no meaning or significance at all, other than an element of confusion that further distorts the perspective of the recent UFO witness. In other cases, the purported MIB visitation is one that could only be described as the summation of terror, and effective in the squelching of any furtherance or proliferation of UFO accounts by the credible witnesses.

The persistent mythos surrounding MIBs is not kept solely to the UFO witnesses, of course. A number of us that are associated with UFO research itself, and the pursuit of answers to the apparent "alien" riddle, find that we are dogged by such encounters, too. While I have never claimed to have any first-hand experiences in this area, the indirect presence of this particular subculture in UFOlogy has nonetheless influenced my own ever-evolving narrative; at times, this influence has been great enough to cause me to wonder about such things as an ongoing conspiracy to silence those who talk openly with researchers about their encounters with the unexplained.

On one occasion, an individual who had claimed to have such an encounter contacted me personally to tell me about their experience with an MIB. As the story went, this person had been leaving work late one evening when they were approached by a short and rather strange looking man, dressed in a black suit. In the distance behind him was a parked vehicle, also black, and though it was a classic make and model, the car was well kept enough to look almost modern in appearance. My contact, while leaving the location, had no choice but to walk directly past the man, who almost seemed intent on standing in the path of anyone operating within the narrow back alley passage, which they now shared uncomfortably.

The story up until this moment had seemed only a bit odd—coincidental, perhaps—but then, as if to match the chill of the evening weather my contact had described for this haunting occasion, I was told what this strange little "man" finally had to say, uttering flatly through a heavy foreign accent: *You are to stop communicating with Micah Hanks, and if you don't, you will see me again.*

One can only guess as to whether stories like this are ultimately true or not, though with time, most any ufologist who is serious about their research into unexplained aerial phenomenon and other odd happenings will begin to accumulate at least a small number of stories like these. It hardly requires mention here that Redfern's initial collection of MIB-related tales, preceding this present volume, details plenty of tales similar to what I've mentioned already, going all the way back to the early years of modern UFOlogy and its humble progenitors.

We know well of those classics—the truly *bizarre* stories told by the likes of Gray Barker and Albert Bender which date back several decades, as well as the kinds of threatening correspondences received privately on several occasions by the late John Keel. In some instances, Keel described unsettling scenarios where he received unstamped envelopes, decorated with red and blue military stripes that gave off an official air, which contained odd messages on anomalous-looking stationary. They ultimately warned that the *Mothman Prophecies* author would meet an untimely fate, should he persist in looking after "matters that didn't concern him."

With certainty, the modern MIB lore cannot be relegated to my own sparse commentary here regarding strange, somewhat diminutive men in suits that threaten UFO witnesses, let alone the letters they are presumed to have written to figures that are now the ghosts of our ufological past. But again to underline the modern counterpart to these decades-old phenomena, another colleague of mine, Greg Newkirk of Canada, wrote publicly in February 2013 about a strange message he received, which bore remarkable similarity to the kinds of odd, "anomalous letters" Keel and others used to speak of. Laden with typos and misspellings so obvious that they might seem *intentional* (perhaps as a measure to disguise the otherwise more attentive grammar and punctuation of a would-be hoaxer?), the message read, simply: *why did you stop when you were so close? I have something for you. one week.*[1]

Whether a distinct parallel can be drawn between odd email messages of this variety and the ongoing menace of the UFO-silencing Men in Black is anyone's guess. But one thing remains obvious throughout even the vaguest obfuscation of details and intentions: a key part of the ongoing effort to derail serious UFO research has been a reliance on absurdity and misdirection, as well as the more widely reported sources of pure intimidation many expect of the MIBs.

As John Keel had surmised in his day, even the more frightening instances of interaction with would-be UFO silencers had their likely roots in the ambiguous activities perpetrated behind the scenes by other UFO enthusiasts. Gray Barker, the very man who penned the famous book *They Knew Too Much About Flying Saucers,* which detailed the first examples of MIB encounters in ufological literature, was supposed by Keel to have been actively engaging in the authorship of "anomalous letters." In addition to penning confusing or scary sounding "phoney" messages to his colleagues, Keel would also note that Barker appeared to have sent him messages bearing his actual name, which nonetheless were addressed erroneously to mutual colleagues of theirs, such as the late Jim Moseley. In Keel's opinion, these were intended to further riddle the perspectives and correspondences of UFO researchers, including Keel himself, with adverse paranoia and confusion.

Following that line of thought for a moment, here it is certainly worth discussing "Dr. Richard H. Pratt," a man also appearing in Barker's aforementioned book, who would later pen an article titled "Gray Barker: My Friend, the Myth-Maker" for *Skeptical Inquirer* magazine. The piece would carry a shocking assertion: that the author, now going by his real name of "John C. Sherwood," not only admitted to being the very same "Dr. Pratt" that Barker had written about years earlier (despite being only eighteen at the time), but also that Barker had knowingly fabricated the entire tale of three "blackmen," as he called them, who famously accosted the fictional doctor. [2]

To be fair, Barker's book also included the otherwise credible description of researcher Albert Bender's visit by three "government agents," who had threatened him with imprisonment if he continued the inquest regarding UFOs with his International Flying Saucer Bureau. Also, Barker would go on to pen future books on UFOs and MIBs as well, in the decades following his sordid tales of intimidation leveled against Bender and his fictional "Dr. Pratt." Among these titles, one would become renowned among the more suspicious and paranoid offerings on the MIB subject: a book which saw only minor circulation at the time of its release, called *MIB: The Secret Terror Among Us.*

Described as "the grand final statement from a master of many genres," what became Barker's final published work (now available in a reprinted edition, with thanks to researcher

Andy Colvin) without question details several of the more intriguing elements regarding the ongoing presence of dark-suited silencers within the annals of UFOlogy.

But strangely, Barker's continued interest in the MIB subject also presents us with something of a "chicken or the egg" argument. Former UFO researcher Bill Moore (who left the field after controversy erupted surrounding MJ-12 documents and his involvement with a so-called intelligence operation dubbed "The Aviary") would claim in the 1980s that MIBs aren't merely government agents in disguise, but that they were also members of an intelligence group called the Air Force Special Activities Center, based out of Fort Belvoir, Virginia. [3] Moore further alleged that stories like the ones Barker had written back in the 1950s had literally been the *inspiration* behind the Air Force's ongoing interest in sending "agents" into the field to investigate the claims of UFO witnesses. [4]

It is indeed a strange concept, that Barker's later writing might have been influenced heavily by reports stemming from government activities... and operations, no less, for which he could also have been the initial inspiration! At its conception, Barker had no doubt reveled in the brilliant urban "folktales" he had partially concocted from pure imagination, in collusion with his then eighteen-year-old friend, merely to instill a sense of dark provocation and exaggerated paranoia behind his already sensational UFO journalism. If anything, it was a subgenre within his greater body of work that Barker himself referred to, rather candidly, as being his "kooky books." [5] But not to allow any of the well-documented misinformation and general saucer-smearing from within the UFO community to derail our examination of the credible MIB reports, perhaps there are yet aspects to this ongoing enigma that would serve our inquiry amidst less social confusion. Tracing the mystery even further back into the realm of myth, religion and folklore, we find that the Man in Black has even deeper cultural roots in other parts of the world, in places where the archetypal ingredients of the modern day MIB recipe are still gardened and grown to this day...perhaps even within a fertile kind of psychological soil that is more pure than what any contemporary ufological scene could afford to offer.

Indeed, the supernatural tradition of the Man in Black is much further reaching than these scant and spurious modern accounts. Jeffrey Burton Russell of the Medieval Studies Institute of at the University of Notre Dame wrote of the inherent conscription of blackness by the purveyors of evil in myth and folklore in his treatise on the master of all sin, *The Devil: Perceptions of Evil from Antiquity to Primitive Christianity*:

Blackness and darkness are almost always associated with evil, in opposition to the association of whiteness and light with good... when Shiva is black, the color represents the evil side of his nature; the color of Kali, the destroyer, is usually black. It is natural therefore that the devil's most common color is black, though he is also frequently associated with red. [6]

Russell then cites clear reasons for why black is the preferred shade to be donned by those carrying out acts of wickedness: Blackness possesses an immense range of negative and fearful associations. Basically black is the color of night, when your enemies can surprise you and when ghosts or nameless, shapeless beings can attack you unexpectedly. Cosmogonically, blackness is chaos; ontogenically, it is the sign of death and the tomb, or of the ambivalent womb. Though pallor is associated with death and hence with evil - heretics and demons are often pallid in the Middle Ages - black indicates evil in places as disparate as Europe, Africa, Tibet, and Siberia, and recent experiments with American children seem to show a prejudice against the color black separate from racial attitudes. [7]

Peter M. Rojcewicz further expounded on the pattern associations that can be drawn between folkloric manifestations of evil and UFOlogy, choosing to make the MIB character the chief focus of his paper, "The 'Men in Black' Experience and Tradition: Analogues with the Traditional Devil Hypothesis." In it, he argued that the interrelationship between UFOs and folklore is best exemplified in the stories of the MIB encounter:

Most existing folklore studies of UFO belief materials have failed to fully appreciate the complex interrelatedness of UFOs with numerous belief traditions. This fact is no more clearly demonstrated, perhaps, than with belief in the "Men in Black" (MIB). The MIB phenomenon constitutes a rather esoteric part of the UFO experience and tradition. The cryptic nature of the MIB indicates something of the complexity of the UFO question, as it involves a continuum of related but discrete phenomena and beliefs. [8]

At times what can be considered an evil, otherworldly, or even *inhuman* theme (something of a "continuum," as described above) often does arise in reports of the classical "Man in Black" encounter, and the folkloric parallels, as Rojcewicz notes, are quite strong in the modern MIB literature. Contemporary reports given by alleged MIB witnesses will, time after time, relate encounters with awkward "people," whose skin may seem discolored or waxy in texture; they also seem to prolifically employ wires and other odd accoutrements around the neck, wrists and ankles, perhaps evidence of wire-tapping devices or concealed recorders. And even their manner of speaking appears to seem foreign, variously described as being laden heavily with accent, or with odd, mechanical tones that strike the ear as being unnatural.

This was even the case in the instance related to me by one of my contacts that claimed to have a face-to-face encounter with a MIB. If it is to be taken literally, perhaps the strangest element to the entire ordeal had been how the witness recounted that, even in the cold weather of a late winter evening, the individual who warned about speaking to UFO researchers like me had apparently produced no natural fog of breath as his words struck the chilly air. Again, one can only guess if such observations point to anything deeper underlying the strange MIB mystery. And yet deeper questions are the very stuff of our attempt at understanding this curious puzzle, as answers may yet again lie in whether the MIB phenomenon can truly be so simply defined as a constant, modern enigma related solely to UFO sightings.

As the astute Fortean and ufologist Jerome Clark told *Slate.com* in May of 2012, some of the MIB experiences in modern times literally appear to be of the variety that, "don't seem to have occurred in the world of consensus reality." Looking toward the extremes, it may indeed be a stretch to assert that UFOs are anything as far-fetched as literal "time travelers," for instance, like Gray Barker and his youthful associate "Dr. Richard Pratt" elucidated for the apparent purpose of mere trickery so many years ago.

Still, to acknowledge that an ongoing association exists between archetypal portrayals of evil throughout time, and the present day manifestations of "Men in Black," shows us two things: first, that whatever actually constitutes the MIB mystery, and despite what levels of perception or existence it operates within, it is not something that in any way appears friendly. But perhaps even more unsettling is the notion that this is a variety of phenomenon that may literally have been *created by us*, to some extent, whether by mere imagination, or through inspiration fueled by the propaganda surfacing in the convoluted UFO literature of the past few decades.

Indeed, the final perceptual manifestation known in our culture today as the nefarious "Men in Black" could be something far stranger than any of us have taken time to fully grasp or envision.

Sources:

Newkirk, Greg (Author). Web log post. Facebook.com. February 4. Web. (Accessed February 20, 2013). http://www. facebook.com/photo.php?fbid=10151306825209440&se t=a.438110054439.224401.512199439&type=1

Sherwood, John C. "Gray Barker: My Friend, the Myth-Maker". *Skeptical Inquirer.* May/June 1998.

Clark, Jerome. *The UFO Encyclopedia, volume 3: High Strangeness, UFO's from 1960 through 1979.* Omnigraphis. 1996. Ibid.

Sherwood, John C. "Gray Barker's Book of Bunk: Mothman, Saucers, and MIB". *Skeptical Inquirer.* May/June 2002.

Russell, Jeffrey Burton. *The Devil: Perceptions of Evil from Antiquity to Primitive Christianity.* Cornell University Press. 1977. Ibid.

Rojcewicz, Peter M. "The 'Men in Black' Experience and Tradition: Analogues with the Traditional Devil Hypothesis." *The Journal of American Folklore.* Vol. 100, No. 396 (Apr-Jun, 1987), pp. 148-160. http://www.jstor.org/discover/10. 2307/540919?uid=3739776&uid=2&uid=4&uid=3739256& sid=21101838765407

Harris, Aisha. "Do UFO Hunters Still Report "Men in Black" Sightings?" Slate.com. May 23, 2012. Accessed February 19, 2013. http://www.slate.com/blogs/browbeat/2012/05/23/ men_in_black_sightings_do_they_still_happen_.html

19.

"Feeling a little paranoid
I quickened my pace"

In 2011, the following, extraordinary account was provided to me by a British man named Tim Cowell, who is a freelance videographer filming professionally since 2008. He has a Bachelor of Arts Honors degree in Film, Television and Advertising from the University of Wales, Aberystwyth. His filming credits include Fashion TV, corporate businesses, Wrexham council, the education sector and various documentaries. Alongside his freelance work he is currently studying for his second degree in Creative Media Technology at Glyndwr University. He also volunteers his photography skills to Wrexham County Borough Museum and Archives. Tim Cowell lives in Wrexham, North Wales. Tim's account demonstrates that whoever, or whatever, the Men in Black may be, they were as active in the 1990s as they were when the likes of poor Albert Bender were being terrorized back in the early 1950s. Notably, as our correspondence progressed, Tim revealed that – MIB aside - he had lifelong experience of strange phenomena, including encounters of both a ghostly and a Ufological kind. Just like Albert Bender, in fact...

The reason I am writing to you is in regards to a strange experience I had back in 1997 when I was 17 years old. Whether you may be able to shed light on my experience, I'm not sure, but I came across your name and "real men in black" article on the web a few moments ago and felt that your expertise on the subject might lift a nagging uncertainty that I have had for fourteen years.

Firstly, I would like to say that I have not read your "men in black" book as yet (I do intend to) but I do have an interest in the unexplained and have read many books on these subjects since I have had multiple strange experiences in my past and present. That being said, the experience I wish to convey to you has not been contaminated with any theories of others or my own.

I am very open-minded but at the same time possess a healthy skepticism with any unexplained phenomena. However, I have not found any logical reason for what I am about to tell you (although there is always the possibility that there is one). The following account is complete truth and I have not embellished any part of it. All I hope is that you might have an explanation for what happened, be it strange or mundane, as I am uncertain as to whether this account depicts the behavior of the "Men in Black"? At the time of the experience I was 17 years of age and was "bunking off" from a college lecture to meet my then girlfriend later that afternoon...

My Account: I was walking from my college and into town to get a coffee to pass the hour until I caught the bus to my girlfriend. I was young and newly "in love" and walking quite happily down the main street when I had a strange feeling that I was being followed. This feeling led to an instinct of looking behind me and as I did, a few feet away, I saw a couple of men close behind. As I looked they both emitted a "blank" smile. Being young and - dare I say it - possibly naive, I had the thought that maybe they were from the college and following me because I bunked off. (On reading this whole account you will see that what happened is not the normal procedure any college would take.)

After I witnessed this "blank smile" I continued to walk at my normal pace down the long main street towards my destination. I was now wondering to myself if they smiled at me because I looked at them (the old "you look at me so I look at you" scenario). I looked behind me a second time and again they offered, in unison, that same blank smile. I also noticed their appearance and whilst they were not wearing black suits and black fedoras, they were wearing an attire that didn't seem to fit in. Dark brown tweed suits with matching long over-coats and fedora-like hats. Without sounding clichéd (as I now know the usual nonconformity of these guys) they did appear to be from an earlier era than the '90's, to say the least.

I decided to quicken my pace and noticed that their pace also quickened. Feeling a little paranoid I quickened my pace again; and again they also matched my speed. So now I'm almost speed walking towards the cafe to get my coffee. A third look behind me before I entered (the then) "John

Menzies" [a British store-chain] confirmed that they were still walking my way so I entered the store but waited inside a little for them to pass by. They didn't, so I ventured into the street again but they had disappeared. I immediately assumed that they had turned off or entered another shop and put it down to myself as being a paranoid college bunker.

I re-entered the store and proceeded to walk upstairs to the cafe area. It is worth mentioning here that whilst I chose this cafe for its quietness it did always bug me that the cafe attendants rarely gave you enough time to choose what you wanted without being quickly pestered into hurrying up with your order. (The reason for this note will become apparent soon). Having being quickly served at the counter, I found a place to sit at a table facing the cafe entrance and began to read a letter that my girlfriend had sent me (sickening I know).

Anyway, a few moments later I looked up from the letter whilst taking a sip of my coffee and froze on the spot. The two distinguished gentlemen were a few feet away at the food counter staring at me blankly. After what seemed like an age of staring, one of the men placed a large leather-like satchel on the floor. I hadn't even noticed it before.

With the other man still looking at me, the other bent down, opened the satchel and pulled out a very large and old looking camera, complete with large round flash. He proceeded to point the camera directly at me and took my picture. On doing so he placed the camera back in the satchel and both men turned and slowly walked away towards the stairs.

Completely in shock and bemused as to what just happened, I was still frozen in place trying to wonder what the hell had just happened. I quickly decided to follow them (the time taken for this decision, taking into consideration the casual speed at which they exited, I calculated that they would still be going down the stairs or at least at the bottom by the time I got to them) and literally ran down the stairs. There was no sign of them so I decided to go to the store exit first and looked outside but they weren't anywhere to be seen. I then turned to look into the store again due to the fact that I might have missed them inside and that they would have had to pass me to leave. But again they were nowhere to be seen.

One thing that was apparent to me was that whilst they were upstairs by the counter they were never attended to by the very needy cafe staff and believe me they used to pester you. To be honest, without sounding stupid it seemed like no-one could see them. I know how that sounds but all I can do is explain the account in the same way I experienced it.

Now, as a 17 year old bunking off college, I was hesitant to tell my mother of this experience (not because of the ludicrous way it would have sounded - she actually took that part in her stride as she has also experienced strange phenomena in her life), but because I thought I would have been grounded for bunking off. Least to say, when I did arrive home later that day I told her the exact same thing I told you now, including why I was not in college.

The intrigue of my experience swayed the "grounding"

and to this day I have no logical reason as why something like that would happen to me. Obviously with my interest in all things weird becoming larger and larger over time and the ease as to which information about ourselves can be found out via the Internet, this aspect couldn't have been the reason for this strange occurrence as I was rarely on the new "Internet" back then. Anyway, what happened that day is a mystery and there could be a mundane reason for it. But there are little things that bug me. Why did I feel I was being followed only to see that I was? Why did they seem out of place in both their clothes and their blank demeanor? Why take a picture of me at all, let alone with the most old-fashioned of cameras? And how did they disappear so quickly? Is this the type of behavior that you would deem to be of 'Men in Black' origin?

I know that account sounded a little "wacko" but I assure you I am of sound mind. I simply have an experience that I have no answer for. Thank you for taking the time to read this long-winded email and I hope to hear from you soon. Kind regards, Tim Cowell.

I wrote back to Tim and asked a few questions regarding the specific location, and received the following in response:

Hi Nick, Thanks for your reply. That experience was in my home town of Wrexham, North Wales. Like I said, it's something that I recall from time to time with a nagging uncertainty as to what it actually was and why.

Because I have had many paranormal experiences, I had wondered if there was any link between them. Most of these have been placed in the more ghostly category but there was an incident when I was even younger when myself and grandma witnessed a UFO sighting. The same night of the sighting I was sharing a bed with my cousin (we were being babysat during a weekend) and when I awoke in the morning my Gran found us "artificially" laying in the bed...myself lying on my back with arms crossed neatly over my chest and my cousin upside down, feet on the pillow and head under the quilt at the bottom. Not a normal way to sleep and the bed sheets were as if they had been made whilst we were already in them. Strange.

All through my life I've seen, felt and heard "ghosts" - or whatever - in my family home and even more recently encountered paranormal resistance whilst living and working in Malta that required the help of a Catholic priest! I'd love to write a book about my experiences but don't know the first thing about publishing :)

Anyway, whilst I have and continue to experience strange things, I simply had no explanation at all as to who those strange men who followed me were. The only reason I have regained interest in that strange day was thanks to a movie that I had recently watched call "*The Adjustment Bureau*". In the same way that smelling a scent can transport to back to a memory, I had the same jolt of surprise when I saw these "adjustment men" in that movie as their appearance instantly reminded me of that day back in 1997. Thus thrusting me back onto the internet to try and find anyone with an answer or similar experience to mine.

And that's when I came across your book, "*The Real Men In Black*". I have to say that I do own your book *Cosmic Crashes* and because I enjoyed it and realized that you were the same author I ventured to ask you your opinion on the matter. Again, thanks for your reply and I feel better knowing that an author of your caliber and experience on the subject appreciates the weird and wonderful. Kind regards, Tim Cowell.

20.

"The voices revealed themselves as the MIB"

"Dean Francis" has, for many years, studied both UFOlogy and cryptozoology. At the time of his encounter with the MIB – a story that he tells below – Dean was heavily involved in spiritualism, Reiki, and séances. I will leave it up to the reader to decide if this involvement has a bearing upon the Men in Black aspect of Dean's experiences…

Firstly a little bit about myself: I was brought up a spiritualist since the age of 15. I am now 30 and have always had an interest in UFOs since an early age, even before I got into spiritualism. My involvement in spiritualism lasted a good 5-10 years to the point where I got into Spiritual healing, Reiki and even some Physical Phenomena séances, which were held in the dark where spirits from the other side would come through and speak and also physically materialize and touch people. All this looking back now could be seen as the occult, a subject which you brought up in *Final Events*.

After speaking about my sighting/encounter on that fateful day in Belgrave with some close friends many years ago, things started changing. I quite often got the feeling of being followed which slowly increased and became worse. After 2-3 years of these feelings, it became a mental strain on my life to the point where I quit my job and became a recluse.

One year later I found that I was severely ill, as I started hearing voices; these voices, little did I know, became so extreme that I was hearing them all the time to the point where they started tormenting me. Eventually the peg broke and the voices revealed themselves as the MIB and they asked me whether or not I would like to join them. In order to do so I would have to pledge my soul to them. I said NO, and with that went to a mental health clinic to receive some help, which I am now fine and have been fine for some years.

I have no doubt in my mind that the MIB ruined my life and are a Demonic force in nature and as your book implies that they are there to guide people away from the true God. Your book *Final Events* where it talks about them wanting to harvest souls is true and it struck a core with me as you can gather from my own experience.

I have also given spirituality the flick and am no longer involved with it and have decided to become a Christian, as I believe whole heartedly that most people in spiritualism are deluded, misguided individuals. I never saw spiritualism as the occult before but I do now.

I could probably write more but don't have the motivation to do so. A lot happened in those years that I have not written. I have just given you a very small breakdown of what happened. Feel free to use my story in any which way or form, in fact I'd be happy for you to spread the message that UFOs and those associated with them are demonic.

. . . .

UFO Sighting. Location: Belgrave, Vic, Australia.
Date: Between the 24/10/97 and 5/5/98.

. . . .

I have a list of 5 dates that it would have occurred on. They are as follows, 24/10/97, 4/12/97, 8/1/98, 30/3/98, and 5/5/98. I have based these possible dates of the sighting on the day of a personal friend's doctor's appointment. I seem to recall saying to myself after the event that I would never forget the date, as it was a major sighting; obviously I have. I am sure it fell on, or was close to, a personal anniversary or major date of some sort. I will continue to investigate and narrow the day down further.

I used to live in a small town on the outskirts of Belgrave called Belgrave Heights in the outer eastern suburbs of Melbourne, Australia. I don't know if anyone knows the area well, but Belgrave is where the sighting occurred. It's probably best known for its tourist attraction "Puffing Billy," an old steam locomotive which runs through the Dandenong Ranges, and also for its laidback, alternative lifestyle. In the centre of town on the low side of the main street, you have a collection of shops, then behind them the railway line and on the high side, you have more shops. Above them, there is a car park which links up with the local supermarket and library and has nice panoramic views South-East over towards Narre Warren East and Cardinia Reservoir way.

Anyway, I was sitting in the car, in the car park, waiting for a friend to come back from her doctor's appointment. It was just getting on dusk and I was admiring the views over the valley towards the South-East when my attention turned to a bright star, or what I thought to be a bright star, on the horizon in the distance. I thought it odd at the time because it seemed a little too bright (which was an orange-yellow color, more of an orange than a yellow) in regards to the stars around it, which were only just starting to come out.

I kept looking at this star for about 1 to 2 minutes thinking it's brightness odd, until zip (excuse the sound effects) it flew off at incredible speed, almost straight up and out of sight. It was gone in less than a second. At this point my full attention was on this one spot on the horizon and as a minute or so passed, I thought that that was it. This bright star like object that seemed to fly at an impossible speed may have gone. Until suddenly, almost out of nowhere, the same one or another one appeared. This one didn't fly in. It was just there, as if turning on a light. Then another flew in at "very" high speed, and before I knew it, another had appeared.

I would estimate the area at which I believe I saw these craft to be huddled to be around the South East to South South-East of my position, probably an area near or close to Cardinia Reservoir in Emerald.

I was suddenly watching these lights come and go at

incredible speeds, appear and disappear as if turning a light on and off, and then I watched as one of them did aerial aerobics that zigzagged across a small section of the horizon, only to watch another chase it playfully.

While this aerial aerobics was going on, one of them then proceeded to move at a steady pace (around the same speed as a light aircraft would travel if it was sightseeing) from its South South-East position to the West North-West Position. I watched this light move right across the horizon to the south of me until it was out of sight. I watched three of them move across the horizon, the last one being very close to my position.

I then returned my gaze back to the others that were still there. At this point, they were accompanied by not another one, but another two or three. Zip again, another flew off, straight up, and was gone in a flash.

As I am writing this report 8-9 years later, I will write in all honesty that what I have written so far in regards to the comings and goings of the craft, how many there were at any one time etc. may be a little off. (This is only in regards to the craft that remained on the horizon doing their aerial aerobics, but basically what I have written so far is as close to a representation of what occurred as I can get). The three that moved across the horizon did happen as described.

The three that proceeded to move across the horizon moved (one at a time) from a South South-East position to a North Westerly position and as each one moved, the one after would move a little more north. Each craft always waited for the other to move right across the horizon before the other would move.

I remember thinking that it seemed like they were scanning the area. It was almost like they were mapping the surrounding area out, to create some sort of geological database as each one never followed the other.

I must also comment on the fact that when they moved to a more suburban built up area, the bright orange-yellow light that they were emitting would suddenly go out and you were left with a series of flashing lights that could have very easily been mistaken for a normal light aircraft such as a plane, as they had the same characteristic flashing light patterns. I found this rather clever.

Were it not for the fact that I had witnessed that very same craft perform its aerial aerobics, and change its color from its orange-yellow to a series of flashing lights, you could have very easily mistaken it for just that, a light aircraft. Making most people totally ignore or be oblivious to it. I remember counting around nine or more aircraft all up from the experience, all the same bright orange-yellow color.

Now this is where it gets interesting, because they were moving slowly north and getting closer to my position sitting in the car park. It's an experience I will never ever forget! I sat in total amazement as one of them was flying in my direction. I was about to view a UFO in very close proximity. I had always dreamt of seeing one of these things close up and now

I was getting the chance. The anticipation of watching this thing draw near was quite spellbinding to say the least.

Now these details people may find hard to believe, but I will not hold back. I will express my own truth to the events of what I saw and the feelings that I got or felt from the experience. As it drew nearer to my position I saw it suddenly change color, from its bright orange-yellow to a very dark indigo-black. It was almost like switching off a force field of bright light to show its true shell underneath, a dark matt metallic color, which made it blend in very well with the night sky. Again it was obviously trying to stay more inconspicuous in a more suburban built up area. I watched in disbelief as it flew straight over the Safeway supermarket car park, then almost directly over the library cutting across the car park I was sitting in, to fly over the church and out of sight. All this happened no more than 50-60 meters away from me. I was able to see the whole craft in full view.

It was your typical saucer shaped craft; I would estimate the length to be around 30-40 meters wide and was of a dark indigo-black color. The blackness may have been a trick of light as it was getting quite dark by this time. But it definitely had a dark blue tinge to it and was certainly nothing like the bright orange-yellow color it was displaying earlier. I was able to make out some small colored flashing lights that ran in a circular motion on the outermost underneath part of the craft. The exact colors escape me but they ranged from blues, yellows, reds, and whites there may have been others, maybe a green, I can't really remember now, but at the time, this was not the focus of my attention. As I was able to see large portholes or windows that surrounded the outermost part of the craft. Through them, the shadowy outlines of humanoid figures peered out.

I was able to decipher two distinct humanoids, a taller and a smaller. The first that I noticed was that of the taller humanoids, they stood out because of their size. They were just standing there peering out the windows with arms by their sides. I was able to see them from just above the head, to just below the waist line, and the more I focused in, not really believing what I was seeing, the more I realized that they were "very human looking". As to my surprise, I could make out that they were wearing dark suits and ties! Something we are quite accustomed to seeing here on earth.

Looking around some more, I saw the shadowy outlines of the smaller humanoids. Only their heads were visible and they too were just peering out the windows. They were half the size in height in regards to the taller humanoids, but then I realized that their heads were larger, almost 2-3 times as large! They had no hair on their head and I could just make out some large, dark, almond shaped eyes. It then occurred to me that I was looking at one of the famous Grays, which are heard of so often in sighting reports around the world. I was not able to make out fine facial features as there was a light source coming from behind the occupants.

I was able to make out some of the décor inside the craft,

which was rather plain looking, which surprised me as I was expecting to see something that would have been totally 'alien' in appearance. You know, maybe some strange or abnormal architecture or at least some unknown colors or lights. I saw nothing of the sort. In fact, the feeling that I got of the décor was that it had a 60s to 70s office-building feel?

I was able to see what looked like wooden or wood veneer walls, as I could make out the grain in the wood, and it was that of or what seemed to be a light oak which had a dark tan color. They ran in large vertical panels down the wall. I also remember seeing what looked like maroon color pin board material walls or curtains. The wooden walls immediately reminded me a lot of walking into a high-ranking governmental type building, but with that strange 60s-70s feel. Also, I seem to have a strong memory of seeing fluorescent lighting on the roof, the ones which have those squared crisscross reflectors that are usually made out of silver plastic to reflect more light!

The roof was of a light grey-white or cream color. The roof also looked as though it was made out of that cork board material or something to that effect, as it seemed to be put together in sections. Again something you usually see in an office type environment? The décor just seemed out of place for something that you would associate with flying saucers, which is why it stood out so much and really, talking about it now, shouldn't have looked "earthly" at all. I found all this rather odd.

What was I seeing, Men in Suits, standing and flying

alongside the Grays! Thoughts rushed through my head. Is this the government working alongside the Grays or is it the military? Or are these men in suits just some sort of hybrid race working anonymously with the Grays and without the government or military knowing? Or am I looking at the famous Men in Black? The thoughts kept coming; I just couldn't believe what I was seeing.

Focusing my attention back to one of the Grays, I sensed a certain amount of calmness and peace radiating from it. It had a kind of strong "presence" which could be "felt" just by looking at it. It seemed to be radiating a constant state of euphoria or ecstasy.

Each humanoid was standing solitary at its very own window, and I must have seen at least 3-4 humanoids in suits and about 2-3 Grays. Most of the Grays were standing at the front area of the saucer. By that I mean the area that one would stand if you were flying the craft; whether or not this is where you would fly that craft is unknown of course, but nevertheless was an observation. Because I was only able to see one side of the craft, there may have been more humanoids standing at the windows on the other side.

This craft made no sound whatsoever and was very low to the surrounds, probably around 50-60 meters of the ground when it flew past me, which is why I got a good look at it and its occupants.

I did not have any feelings of lost time, although I did have a strange feeling that time may have stalled momentarily while it passed over. Thinking about that later, it occurred to me that maybe because of the strong anti-gravitational electro magnetism of the craft (I am guessing that's what is used in anti-gravity), it might have been able to distort or confuse the electrical impulses of the brain, therefore creating a strange stalled time effect. I have heard of UFOs disrupting electrical equipment as they fly over areas, stalling cars for instance and interfering in radio waves, etc. I remember making the effort to look at the clock after it was gone, just to make sure that I was not missing any time and all was normal. Although I am writing this report 8-9 years later, I am unable to determine or remember the exact time of the sighting. I only know that it was at dusk.

I don't know if they knew that I could see them or not, and I got no telepathic communication from any of them, just the strong feeling of peace and euphoria radiating from one of the Grays. I did not find any unusual scars or come down with any strange symptoms of sickness and do not believe anything untoward happened. It just drifted straight over the car park and out of sight.

I probably saw it (close up) for about 30 seconds before it flew Northwest at a steady pace over the hill, certainly enough time for me to comprehend what I was seeing. Although the technology of this craft was far beyond what we are used to seeing here on Earth, like being able to move and fly about erratically at incredible speeds, change colors from bright orange-yellow to become almost invisible in its surrounds, and fly in complete silence. It also had some strange earth like characteristics like 60–70s décor, and then what looked like fluorescent lighting.

At the time I got a feeling that the craft seemed rather "earthly." Just a feeling I suppose. From seeing the first UFO on the horizon over towards Cardinia Reservoir, to watching the last one fly over the car park and out of sight, was probably around 25 minutes.

I also have a memory of hearing a helicopter flying around the very next night. I remember it raining or having possibly thunder stormed either the night of the sighting (2-3 hours after sighting) or the night after. I'm pretty sure it was the night after. I have that memory because I was going to go outside again the very next night to see if I could see anything but couldn't, probably because it was raining.

I was not under the influence of any drugs whatsoever and I have only presented the facts as I saw them. You may make up your own conclusion to the events. I do not care if anybody believes me or not; it really doesn't bother me. For all those skeptics out there, I will gladly take a polygraph test.

21.

"His eyes were black and his skin a Mediterranean olive"

Lucy Palmer is a former security officer and a Wiccan who runs an occult-supplies store in Manchester, England. Lucy shares with us the unsettling story of Shelagh and her partner, Robert, and their disturbing immersion into the fraught domain of the Men in Black…

They lived together as partners since meeting in 1983, when the paranormal experiences began almost immediately. At the time, Robert was working in a supermarket and Shelagh was at home alone. It was August 1991 and Shelagh was in the kitchen when she heard the front door bell ring. The building was a terraced house on a very busy Oxford Road in Reading [England]. The house had a flight of seven or eight stone steps up to the front door. This was the kind of house with another set of steps leading to a below street level basement room.

Shelagh went to the front door. It had a large pane of frosted glass in it, meaning you could see the shadow of anyone standing outside. But what struck Shelagh was that she could not see the dark form of anybody waiting outside, so her initial thought was that they might have gone down to the basement door.

She opened the door and was confronted by a man with a broad smile on his face, so the suggestion was that he had been standing outside but cast no shadow on the glass! He wore an immaculate black suit, white shirt and black tie. She described his suit as "too perfect to be real, with perfect creases in the legs."

She reported his shirt as a very dazzling white, hypnotically so. She particularly noticed that he didn't have a single bead of sweat on his face or staining his shirt collar, even though it was a very hot, cloudless day. His eyes were black and his skin a Mediterranean olive. He carried a brand new briefcase in his right hand. Shelagh was a former police officer, having served in the Rhodesian Special Branch in the 1950s and 1960s. With her experience she has on many occasions demonstrated a good sense of recall, which is why she took all this visual information in the first moments of confronting him.

Then the weird part of her report is that although the road behind him was a busy main road leading directly into the heart of Reading, she gradually became aware of no traffic and no pedestrians passing, with this, everything behind him seemed to slip out of focus. He, on the other hand, still smiling inanely, became sharper-focused and she could do nothing about it. Shelagh says her vision was restricted, against her wishes, to focus only on his presence.

She could see a small metal pin badge on his right suit jacket lapel and realized this item was what she was continuing to stare at. It sounds like it was exerting a hypnotic fascination. Shelagh never was able to describe what the badge was because, even though she was concentrating on it, she found it challenged her by continually slipping out of focus. He then spoke. He had an accent, foreign, probably European, but she could not place it.

"Hello, is Robert in?"

"No, he's at work."

"Oh ok," the MIB replied, "When is he home?"

"Probably about 6 this evening."

The MIB continued to smile as something very strange happened. It was like a sudden jump in a film because the next moment he was stood two steps further down, but he hadn't physically moved.

Still smiling he then told her: "You do need to stop what you are doing."

Then the jump happened a second time and he was stood down on the pavement, all the time perfectly motionless with hands and briefcase held rigidly at his side. Still smiling and looking up at her. Then the next "jump" and he had turned to face the left, (her right). Then he started to walk away - this being his first actual physical movement that she was aware of.

The moment he was out of sight, she stepped out of the porch expecting him to be walking along the pavement or getting into a car - but he had disappeared. At that point she realized the street sounds had returned and the usual stream of traffic had resumed. She walked along the street, looking down the only side-road close by, but didn't see him, or him in any vehicle. She told Robert about this when he got home and it was documented as another weird encounter. There was no follow up and he never returned physically.

Shelagh had a long history of remarkable clairvoyance, in the 60s she had been a High Priestess in a Wiccan coven; her occult presence was long and experienced. In the 1970s she appeared to undergo an abduction experience. Then when she met Robert in the early 1980s, they received many communications from spirit guides alluding to a "mission." This messaging, received through Shelagh as the medium, was accompanied with a string of paranormal events - the MIB being just one of them.

22.

"It occurred to me that I could make contact with the MIB"

John St. Clair is a graduate of Cornell University in Mechanical Engineering. There he became very interested in Einstein's Theory of Special Relativity. Before this, he won first prize in the Puerto Rico National Science Fair with a project in solar energy.

He nearly burned up in flames the Fresnel lens furnace when removing it from the van below the noonday sun.

He built the first man-carrying ground effect hovercraft in Latin America. Working at Kodak's Optical and Apparatus Division, John obtained several inventions in film and slide projectors…

I went to see the Will Smith and Tommy Lee Jones movie about the Men in Black (MIB). The movie was entertaining, yet the portrayal of the MIB as secret government agents I thought was incorrect. Then I read Nick Redfern's book, *The Real Men In Black* that documented many cases about witnesses who had come in contact with these mysterious MIB beings. Redfern found government documents through the

Freedom of Information Act (FOIA) that showed that government agents were themselves asking who these beings were. So in the beginning when this phenomenon began, they could not have been government agents. Thus the premise of the movie was just a vacuous Hollywood script.

In the second chapter of Redfern's book, he analyses several theories as to who the MIB are and what they are doing here on Earth. He lists hallucinations, hoaxes, tulpas and vampires, tricksters, civilian investigators, G-Men, time travelers, and demons and the occult as possible explanations. Each one seemed plausible, but how to decide?

Then it occurred to me that I could make contact with the MIB and ask them directly all the questions that needed answering. Go to the source, I thought. I could use my remote viewing capabilities and establish contact with the MIB and have them tell me why they are contacting witnesses who have seen UFOs. Why are they dressed in black? How do they appear and disappear suddenly? How can they walk through walls? What is their method of operation? Are they naturally evolved beings and where do they come from? Are they here to harm or help us?

By talking with the MIB, many concepts that have been misunderstood by humanity are now clear and understandable.

Greetings from the MIB: "Dear Human Beings from the MIB Project Manager for Earth: The MIB are here on your Earth with peaceful purposes. We are a galactic race of beings who provide protection from harmful spiritual energy beings.

Due to your physio-energetic nature, humans are suscepti-
ble to invasion by these unwanted energy beings. They want
your energy and body. We are here to see that this invasion is
stopped before any harm can come to you. This book explains
in more detail our method of operation. Thank you, over and
out. MIB Project Manager for Earth."

The wormhole connects another dimension with ours. It
enables the aliens to move between dimensions. You can think
of it as a doorway. How this doorway is formed from space-
time curvature is detailed in the chapter about the Magnetic
Vortex Wormhole Generator. The opening of the wormhole is
filled with low-density white hyperspace mist that makes the
wormhole look like a regular cloud.

In fact, I had some man call me who said that he saw a
UFO go into a cloud and it never came back out. He claimed
that the UFO was hiding in the cloud! So I explained that
what he really was seeing was the opening of a traversable
wormhole with low-speed of light hyperspace energy flowing
out of the other dimension into our dimension. The UFO was
long gone into another dimension.

Because the MIB are here to help us, they do not directly
threaten the witness. They ask the witness about his sighting, getting all the details and recommending that he forget
about it. In the conversation, they then throw in this non
sequitur about how brakes on cars can sometimes malfunction. The human mind then takes this as a mildly disguised
threat if the witness were to reveal something. The situation

is puzzling because how could a simple sighting evoke such a threatening reaction.

After hushing the witness, the MIB walk back out of dimension through the wormhole from which they had appeared. If the witness follows them, their sudden disappearance is also baffling. The MIB Project Manager said that they wear black clothes because it makes them difficult to see when traversing the wormhole from our space to hyperspace. There is a light in the co-dimension that shines through the opening so the MIB can see the entrance.

Many witnesses erroneously think that this light is emanating from a landed UFO. Even though the MIB wear a white shirt, when they turn around all you see is black. From my personal experience, a figure walking between dimensions is only seen as a black silhouette. The human eye can only see a short distance into this hyperspace region. In one case, I had to tell the being when I was able to see her as she walked between dimensions. When I shouted out that I could see her, she knew how close she could be but still remain invisible while looking into my room. In a case where the spacecraft enters unobserved, then the wormhole will dissipate and close naturally.

It is when the wormhole remains open, due to the activity of the witnesses, that problems start happening. In other dimensions there are energy beings that can come into this dimension and cause us spiritual harm. These entities could be demonic energy entities of erratic frequency and low energy.

I encountered a foot-long rod creature that sucked out the hyperspace energy from my 4th green heart chakra energy vortex. The next day I developed chronic fatigue syndrome (CFS), a well-known medical condition. This entity can take possession of your body while suppressing your own energy.

The last reference is a fascinating experience with none other than the Biblical demonic being called Beelzebub. Beelzebub killed all the tropical fish in an indoor pond by poisoning the fish flakes a friend of mine was feeding them. Fortunately I had developed a means of ascending demonic beings into angelic beings by boosting their energy and converting them to a single frequency. The MIB are here to provide protection from these types of unholy situations.

But of course, some entities slip through. I remember reading about a little boy who was playing with a friend of his. The boy started playing with his father's gun, and shot his friend dead.

The little boy said, "I didn't pull the trigger."

My explanation for this is that the entity wanted to create emotional turmoil in the people involved in order to boost its energy and possibly harvest the friend's energy field. So the entity pulled the trigger. Our judicial system needs to recognize what is really going on in these cases.

The MIB Manager told me that their planet is located in this dimension within our galaxy. They operate on many planets whose inhabitants require protection. For example, a whole village might see the UFO and keep talking about it.

The MIB have to go in and hush up the villagers before word gets out to other villages. The Manager went on to say that the MIB are naturally evolved beings. Their planet is similar to that of Earth except that it has a 50/50 water/land ratio. They are not time travelers from the far future, but travel within a limited local time range. In this way they can obtain new, but older model cars from decades ago.

At the end of the conversation, he said goodnight and I asked him if he was finished working for the day. He said in an annoyed tone that, no, he still had to deal with all these bureaucratic papers such as MIB agent reports, project status and accounting that had to be sent to the home planet. He commented it was much more fun to roam the galaxy and explore new things. I guess that things don't change that much after all! MIB – Men In Bureaucracy.

But the question still remains as to how the MIB generate the wormhole in the first place? How do their spacecraft achieve lift without rockets? One of the clues can be seen in Redfern's book, *The Real Men In Black*. One UFO investigator spotted a MIB and followed him down a corridor. The MIB then turned the corner down another hallway. When the investigator turned the corner, he found that the MIB had just disappeared. The length of the hallway was such that the MIB should still have been able to be seen, but that wasn't the case. The MIB was gone. The investigator continued walking along the hallway and came upon an intense electrical field that sent electrons running up and down his body.

So here is the clue that indicates how they create the wormhole. It turns out it can be understood from Einstein's Theory of General Relativity. This understanding leads into many hyperspace devices and capabilities, shown on the right side of the diagram, such as spacecraft propulsion, teleportation, wormhole generation, orbital debris removal, levitation and energy healing. So there is more exciting information in store for the reader as we explore the realm of hyperspace physics, who we really are, and answer all the questions that have puzzled us down through the ages.

In Gray Barker's book, *Men In Black, The Secret Terror* there is supposedly a photograph on page 139 of Indrid Cold. The caption states that this notorious figure could be the head of the MIB! The caption states that this possible photograph of his is unlabelled and unattributed, possibly out of fear. So is this a photograph of him or not? And is he a notorious person?

Well, I happen to have made contact with Indrid Cold. In the Ohio Valley, he landed his spacecraft in the middle of the road, blocking the passage of an approaching car. Indrid then got out and walked slowly toward the man in the car. His arms were folded in front of him and he sported a large smile on his face. I asked Indrid about why he did this and here is what he said: He folded his arms because he did not want the man in the car to think that he was carrying a weapon. He was smiling just to indicate that there was nothing to worry about and that he was friendly. It was to show that it was a friendly contact, nothing threatening. I ran the permutation function in Mathematics and found that his name spells Coil in DDD or Coil in 3D with the initial R. He confirmed that this was the correct permutation.

His spacecraft was described as a 3D funnel chimney lantern. The base is a sphere on the top of which sits the funnel. The funnel is actually a tapered wire-wound solenoid that creates a magnetic field with a vertical gradient. The bottom is a spherical antenna that emits a wave traveling through the funnel. This combination of magnetic field and electromagnetic field, as seen in the chapter on alien spacecraft, is what creates a space-time curvature to generate lift. Not shown is the tripod landing gear. When I initially did the analysis of this vehicle, I did not understand how it generated lift. Then one day I found myself for some reason winding coils all day long. Then I was looking at the equations when Indrid started talking to me. He gave me some clues but still I did not understand. All of a sudden, a brilliant white flash of light hit me and I then I finally understood how his spacecraft worked. He was laughing his head off at seeing me get hit. I started laughing as well.

Afterwards, he told me that he was an explorer for his planet in this galaxy, sending information back to scientists who were analyzing the data. So this was the reason he was near Point Pleasant, West Virginia. A large wormhole had opened up and demonic entities started coming through. So he, like the MIB, was studying the phenomenon.

23.

"Perhaps the black car was my guardian angel"

From someone who has personally experienced the MIB – Jo Ann Koch, who holds a Bachelor of Arts degree in art and psychology, and who wrote the book *Aliens, Abductions and Other Curious Encounters* – comes the following, turbulent tale…

I have been "visited" since I can remember, as early as age two or three. I'm now a senior citizen and very few people know of my experiences. How would it look if a person who is active in her community came up with such a bizarre story?

About two-and-a-half years ago my experiences escalated. A new group of visitors started coming. They seemed to be doing some kind of experiments or investigations, mostly in my bedroom. The new ones were like greys but I felt they were extremely unpleasant. I was terrified of them and felt that they had no essence.

I began to feel angry and violated and I started to react to them and fight back. After that, they began bringing some type of animal with them. It was about the size of a raccoon and dark brown. Its face resembled a bat except the ears didn't stick up. Rather, they looked like a teddy bear's. Its fur was soft and silky. I was not particularly afraid of it. Instead, I felt comforted by it. It would sit on my neck, to hold me down, but to me it felt like a security blanket.

Finally, one night they came (with their animal) and started using a large needle. They stuck it in my hip (like the bone biopsy I was to have later.) I cannot describe the pain and terror I felt. All the time, of course, my animal friend was there and oddly I felt that he felt sorry for me. In the background there was a large entity dressed in black (an MIB?) I think he had yellow or gold on his chest. He seemed to be the director. Then I slept I think.

The next morning I woke up and remembered the incident but only felt some curiosity as I'm used to things happening. I got out of bed and had to grab the dresser as I had no strength at all: I could hardly stand up. After a couple of hours I was doing fine but I felt that something very deep and fundamental had been taken from me. A conclusion I have drawn from this experience is that they are not really experimenting on us but are harvesting something. They would be pretty dumb to be experimenting on people after all of these generations. They should have learned what they wanted to know by now.

Less than a month later my first symptoms appeared. I got very sick but I thought I had the flu. After about a week I felt better but then I broke out in a rash that covered my entire body. It was curious because the rash consisted of at least three different rashes: red spots, red raised welts, and ulcerations in some spots. Of course I went to the doctor and he cringed when he saw me. He sent me to a dermatologist who prescribed two different ointments. They helped get the rash under control. Strangely, as the rash healed, my body peeled.

Then, the worse began. I got weaker and weaker and was quickly admitted to the hospital when my hemoglobin went down to six. I had an emergency transfusion of two pints of blood. I ended up with five plus doctors and various others who worked on me for eight months.

I had every test imaginable: several scans, heart and lung studies, x-rays and innumerable blood tests. All of my lab tests proved abnormal but nothing definitive. The tests just proved that I was basically healthy. It was at this point that I had a bone biopsy-identical to the treatment I had from the aliens. It, too, proved that I was basically healthy but dying of some undiagnosable illness.

After several more transfusions, the doctors were giving up. I decided that since they were not helping at all, I would try some alternative therapies. I used acupuncture, cranial sacral work and also a chiropractor who did energy healing. I am convinced these modalities saved my life. The medical doctors were doing nothing except giving me transfusions to keep me alive. In fact, I was just days away from having chemotherapy to kill my immune system to see if that would help.

The doctors told my daughter (a doctor) that I was probably dying. I believe that my body was fighting some alien virus and in doing so was also killing my red blood cells. I think that if the chemo had killed my red blood cells, I would have died for sure since that was the last line of defense.

From the first alternative treatments, I began to improve. The chiropractor used energy vials developed by Dr. Randall Frank. I was fortunate enough to be able to meet him because he was visiting from Germany. He did the final healing, and it was a difficult mental and physical experience. Basically I was healed in less than two weeks after months of tests and uncertainties.

It turns out that Dr. Frank does work with UFOs but it is not advertised on his website. My blood count improved quickly and it was up over 10 from the first. My doctors backed off from the chemo. At least three of them told my family that I was a miracle. They asked me what I had done to improve but of course I couldn't tell them that I had gotten help to deal with an alien virus. As with all of my visits, there are times I believe them and other times when I feel I am hallucinating - I am pretty sure that I am not.

After a particularly busy time of abductions and lessons, I went out one morning about 7:00 am for the morning paper. Standing at the end of our driveway was a tall, thin man dressed in a black warm-up suit. The collar was turned up so I couldn't completely see his face but he appeared to be an albino. He had three-inch long, spiky hair that was whitish blond. I wanted to approach him but once he was sure I had seen him, he quickly walked away. I have several neighbors who regularly walk their dogs and no one had seen anyone like him, before or since.

A few days later I again went out about 7:00 am and there was a huge black SUV parked in our driveway. Once I came out it backed away and left with a squeal of tires. This was about 3 years ago and nothing has happened since. I didn't feel threatened, only curious.

I was wondering about another experience I had in the same time frame as the others-give or take a couple of months. I don't know if it falls into the same category because I have not read anything like it.

My husband and I were coming home from a trip and decided to stop in Wrightwood, a popular ski area, especially for cross country skiing. It's less less than two hours from our home. It was summertime and we wanted to see the area. It is a strange little town, only two blocks long, but the area has beautiful large forests. The only thing on t.v. was a religious program and maybe two stations.

We stayed for two days and then headed home. The way down is a typical winding, two lane mountain road. Part way down, I pulled into a turn out so I could take pictures of the wild flowers. I walked about a block back up the road and was happily shooting away when a pick up truck stopped beside me with two men inside.

One man commented on the flowers and then asked me to give him my camera so he could take a picture for me. (My camera is an expensive digital SLR. I do a lot of photography and use it in my art.) Of course (maybe foolishly) I said no thank you. He kept engaging me in conversation but I knew he was playing with me and that, at the very least, I was going to be robbed. (Meantime my husband was back in the car enjoying the scenery and totally unaware of my predicament.) Finally the driver of the car leaned forward-he had been staying out of sight-and I was able to see him clearly. His entire face was horribly scarred - like he had been burned in a fire. I was terrified!

I could tell the first man was getting ready to get out of the truck when a black sports car pulled up behind the truck. It was like a Corvette only larger. The windows were tinted very dark black so I couldn't see who was inside. Both men in the truck were waving for it to drive around them, which could easily have been done as there was visibility for 200 feet. It just stayed there revving its motor. I told the men they'd better leave and I ran back to our car and we were away. Luckily we were heading in the opposite direction. We were the only three vehicles on the road the entire way down the mountain.

This is up there with the two or three most terrifying experiences of my life. Perhaps the black car was my guardian angel.

24.

"What you doing out here all dressed up like that?"

Cal Stubbington, of British Columbia, Canada, provided the following story to me in 2013. It's a case that is made notable by the fact that it pre-dates the MIB phenomenon that has developed since 1947. In fact, it dates back to the 1930s…

I have a MIB story that comes from a pretty good source. 1930s MIB met at a prairie crossroads by a Ukrainian man. Very interesting outcome. It should be noted that the three brothers from Ukraine that were involved in this encounter also encountered incredible strange phenomena on their farm. If you would like to read about it I will relate it as told by one of the brothers.

Sincerely; Cal.

I was told this by a reliable source, a family friend that did not BS. He was one of the three brothers that immigrated to Saskatchewan from Ukraine in the 1930s. These people, I suspect, brought with them some beliefs that resulted in very strange activity on their farm. They had no wives, just three brothers.

Some mornings they would find the horses' manes and tails "BRAIDED" in a very impressive fashion, but so tight that the horses would not allow them to be undone due to pain from pulling, so they cut them off.

One night the brothers awoke to their barn on fire. They fought the fire with water from buckets to no avail: The barn burned to the ground. As morning approached, they went in very tired to wash the smoke and ash from their face and hands. With the smoking ruins of their barn on their minds, they went for a well-earned sleep. When they awoke later that same day, they gazed out at their barn...exactly as it was before it had burned. Or had it really burned? Who knows but it was as it had always been.

In light of these happenings, there was an the MIB occurrence. One of the brothers was walking down the prairie dirt road when he came upon a very clean well-dressed man at a "crossroads." The man wore a black high-class suit with a tail and a fancy stove pipe hat, all black and no dust.

The Farmer said to him, "what you doing out here all dressed up like that? As he spoke those words he was taking from his pocket his corncob pipe to fill and talk a while.

Upon seeing the corncob pipe the MIB said "Oh, what a very nice pipe" as he admired it. The MIB pulled from his pocket a very expensive looking silvery looking pipe and offered to trade if the farmer would.

The old Ukrainian said, "what, this old thing" and quickly traded. This seemed to suffice at ending the conversation as the farmer sped home to show everyone at home. The only amendment that I can think of is when the MIB saw the farmers corncob pipe, the MIB was transfixed by the pipe and appeared to be amazed by it; he wouldn't take his eyes off it.

Apparently, there were other people over for a stay at the time, and they all marveled at the beautiful pipe that had been traded from the MIB. It was proudly put on the fireplace mantle and stayed there as they all went to bed for the night.

When they awoke the next day, apparently the "spell" had been broken because where the beautiful silver pipe had been proudly displayed on the mantle was instead a stick!! Yes, a stick. I am thinking that with the farmer came some hypnotic spell to allow them all to see the silver pipe. Something like the TV show "Goldmind" the mentalist.

The brothers' name was Alex Delawski and he told me this happened. There were more strange things too but this is what he told me.

A side occurrence just happened to me about three days ago. For the last week or so I have been falling asleep with YouTube videos (42 videos) playing about MIB. I was in the back bedroom of my mobile home and I heard a loud knocking on my door. It was the unmistakable sound of a closed fist on the door. I was surprised to see no one and continued to look through the other widows to the entry. There were no tracks in the fresh snow!?

25.

"I will ask you one more time to leave now"

From firsthand eyewitness Leighton Ward, we have a compelling story of Men in Black, thinly-veiled threats, and what may have been some form of secret, underground, military facility in Arizona…

The following event took place in the spring of 1998 around 2pm. The approximate location the event occurred is about 15 miles southeast of the Bill Williams Wildlife Refuge, which is a remote desert area off the Colorado River with the closest town being Parker, Arizona.

Growing up in the small town of Lake Havasu City, you are surrounded by hundreds of miles of open desert with mountain ranges and endless dirt roads that are great for off-roading. The area this event took place is dotted with abandoned mines which we often explored. I was driving my Jeep and my buddy was behind me in his Toyota Land Cruiser.

The road we were on was a dirt road, no different than any other dirt road in the area. The area was fairly flat with a lot of low brush and creosote bushes. I pulled off the right side of the road to look around. There were no signs, no marking, no dirt piles; nothing at all out of the ordinary.

I got out of my truck and waked about 30 feet. I came across a hole about 15' across, I don't know how deep it was but there was no end in sight. This hole was not visible from the road at all because of the low bushes that are all over in this area. The hole went straight down. Since I have seen a lot of mines, I had come to know what the surrounding area of a mine looks like. The area surrounding the mine is always disturbed with dirt piles from the excavation, roads to the mine and often times warning or no trespassing signs and fences.

This particular hole had no disturbances at all. I only found it because I stumbled upon it by accident. I was surprised that there were no signs or safety fences at all. Aside from the natural camouflage of the surrounding bushes there was no attempts made to hide this hole. The only camouflage to hide the hole was the fact that there was nothing at all such as sign or roads to lead you to believe there was a hole there.

Within a minute or two of us seeing the hole, a black suburban with dark tinted windows rolled up on us. We saw it coming up the road but by the time we saw it, it was almost to our location. I have no idea how they knew we were there so quickly. Two men, wearing all black military fatigues, with black hats and black sunglasses, got out of the driver and passenger side. Both were Caucasians about 6' tall carrying side arms.

They shut their doors and simply said, "You need to leave."

Being a bit of a smart ass at times and with no fences or

signs showing private property or no trespassing, I figured the desert was for everyone.

I simply said, "I don't see any signs saying no trespassing." I said it more as a joke because I really don't like to be messed around with so I wanted to see how serious they were.

With no emotion whatsoever the driver simply said: "I will ask you one more time to leave now." He never took his sunglasses off or made any other movements at all.

I got the point and we drove off.

I really did not think too much about it back then because there are a lot of mines out there. I am now 39 and looking back and looking into similar stories, I can now say it was likely not just a mine. If it were a mine, there would have been much more security to prevent injury.

26.

"I was waking up
unhappy and shaken"

Steve Ray lives in Dallas, Texas, and owns DFWNites.com, a website that reviews what "gentlemen's clubs" in the Dallas-Fort Worth area, a website for which I often write. He shares two entertainingly strange stories with us, one involving Steve, and the other concerning a gyrating pole-dancer...

The most traumatic part of what I'm about to describe happened two months ago, but there was a minor encore two weeks ago that I'm still dealing with. These events did happen, and I only noticed the patterns after the fact.

My story begins after I had been listening to old-time radio horror programs for several months. I started to burn out on Autolite spark plugs and tales calculated to leave me in... suspense! So I explored a little more and ran across *The Paracast* and *Para-Talk*, starting with episodes about the Black-Eyed Kids and moving on to the Men in Black. I devoured those episodes and then ordered the MIB books by you and Grey Barker (I'd listened to the LP version *Flying Saucers – Serious Business* when I was a very young child and read *They*

Knew Too Much About Flying Saucers when I was in my early teens, if that matters.)

I have always had a soft spot for possession and had even performed an improvised ritual – adapted from a prohibition in the Malleus Maleficarum – by wearing an animal mask on the first instant of the new millennium and setting off M-80s tied to giant balloons with crepe-paper messages saying "WELCOME THROUGH" and whatnot, all in hopes of rending the veil asunder and letting a wave of demons into our world. So while I was aware and slightly perturbed by the various stories of how paranormal research often led to personal misfortune, I was still intrigued and kept reading in hopes of seeing something ominous.

Around that same time (July 11, 2012), an artist I like, Tony Millionaire, was selling original sketches, and I wanted to buy one. My first choice had already been sold, but there was another showing a non-specific beast snarling from a darkened hedge, its mouth open and fangs on display. I thought, "Ha! How paranormal, a mysterious animal! I'll get it!" Soon after, I saw Matt Howarth, another artist I like, selling a book titled *I Am Lesion* that was illustrated with a creature in a similar snarling pose. It struck me as odd, but I thought little else of it.

I started to have more nightmares, which isn't unusual for me; sometimes I try to induce nightmares by eating food with hot ghost-pepper powder on it before bed. I was waking up unhappy and shaken after a night of stalking and being pursued by shape-shifting murderers, but that was fine in my book.

After a few days of these sleep traumas (7/15/2012), I went downstairs to drive somewhere and saw a black car in the parking lot, but facing away from me. There was an old white man with wire glasses standing next to it, also facing away from me, putting something into the trunk. I did a double-take, then shook it off as wishful thinking for an MIB encounter, because he wasn't in a suit or wearing a fedora, and the car wasn't an old Cadillac, but a black Ford Five Hundred.

I was chuckling at myself as the man got into his car and drove away, when I realized that while he hadn't been in a suit, he had been wearing a black watch cap over a bald head, and that his clothes were odd, like exercise clothes, his shirt velour with red bands over each hip and cargo pants, and while a Five Hundred isn't as archaic as a 1960's Cadillac, it was only in production for three years, ending in 2007, making it a somewhat out-of-date vehicle.

So on 7/18/2012, one week after ordering the picture of the snarling beast, three days after seeing the MIB in the parking lot, I went driving to Fort Worth for a class. On the way there, traffic slowed to a crawl for a good ten minutes, because a woman was out of her car on the left-hand shoulder and stepping in and out of traffic, in 104-degree weather. I thought she was crazy until I saw the profile of a cat under her car bumper. I decided to be a Good Samaritan and help her catch it, because it must be hers, and I figure she must love her cat as much as I love mine.

It turned out it wasn't her cat at all. She had seen a guy in a truck stopped on the median trying to catch it, and she decided to help, but then it scratched him and he left. So she, I, and another lady stalked and coaxed and worked on getting a hold of that cat for twenty or thirty minutes, with traffic whooshing by, the cat hiding on tires and in the engine compartment, panting with its mouth open and fangs exposed, drooling heavily. I thought it was funny that it had the same open mouth and teeth as the picture I'd bought. I got a hand on the cat at one point, but then it darted away

We finally caught the cat in a cardboard box (said cat was maybe four or six months old, with pale fur like a bleached-out calico, and thin), and I decided to be a hero and pay for the vet bills and adopt it, but I didn't know where to take it, so I traded numbers with the lady who had stopped before me. She said she'd take the cat to the vet and have them call.

Twenty minutes later, the vet clinic calls and confirms that I'm taking financial responsibility for the cat, now named "Freeway," after his heroic beginning. I am feeling very proud.

Ten minutes after that, the vet clinic calls back and tells me that Freeway bit the technician and I'll have to pay $750 to have him quarantined for ten days for rabies, or else they'll turn him over to the public health department for testing. I don't know if Freeway has any other problems or if Freeway is just mean, and $750 is a lot to pay for a cat I just met, so I tell them to chop off Freeway's head, which I know is how rabies tests are done. The clinic girl says okay and hangs up. I now feel like a selfish, brutal skinflint.

Then I look up rabies and discover that drooling is one of the symptoms and that it is incredibly contagious, and I remember that I touched Freeway once, and so I call the clinic back to see if I can get the test results when they come back. And the girl says no, because I didn't pay for the quarantine, it's now a private matter between their tech and her doctor, and there's no way I can be informed.

I start to panic and worry that I'm going to have to spend my entire savings to get vaccinated for rabies, because I don't have insurance, and a full series is apparently $10,000.00. Thirty minutes after being a brave hero, I am now facing financial ruin and/or a horrible, mind-destroying death. My life is quite possibly over, and even worse, I can't even be sure I'd be spending the money wisely or not, because this girl says that the contents of Freeway's brain must stay secret. Finally, she connects me to the clinic owner's voice mail, where I beg to be told of the test results.

Now in misery and terror, I go to the emergency room and explain to the doctors what happened and that I need them to say whether I should start the shots or not. They examine me and find no evidence of broken skin, and they tell me to follow up, because this should be a public record – the girl at the clinic is probably wrong about the confidentiality rules. Even better, I can safely wait several days before I need to begin. I'm still stuck with a $450 E.R. bill, and I discovered I was a craven monster too cheap to save a cat's life, so this has turned out to be an absolutely horrible day.

The next day I get called by the owner of the clinic, who tells me that Freeway has been destroyed, and that yes, she will let me know if he was sick. At that point, I realize that I have gotten to see a Man in Black, I encountered a mysterious animal that soon vanished (I had never tried to rescue an animal like that before, ever), and I had my life completely fall apart, all as advertised – but only a little...Freeway's brain tested negative, after all, and I was only out a few hundred dollars. It was like I was getting a sample, a proof of concept.

In a similar vein, I am just getting through the world's smallest insect plague, with a sparse horde of tiny little three-millimeter beetles in my kitchen. I live on the third story of an apartment, but none of my adjoining neighbors have reported anything, which baffled the management, but what's even weirder is that when I first started throwing out the infested food, there was a SINGLE full-sized inch-long cockroach sitting at eye level on the wall next to the toilet. It didn't try to escape when I crushed it; it was just there, like a demonstration that yes, the phenomenon can deliver real bugs, too, just so I know.

I *had* been discounting this mess, saying it "barely qualified," but I no longer think so. While I was writing up this report, I went to Wikipedia to find a picture of the car for you, and the image I clicked on was http://en.wikipedia.org/wiki/

File:Ford500b.JPG, with a license plate that reads "REPOS-SESSOR" across the top.

Naturally, the demonic overtones of that caught my eye, but then I noticed with the license number "RE-00512". 512 is a power of 2, so it leaps out at people who work in IT, but especially because that very morning I'd been having a lengthy discussion with co-workers about lazy programmers who waste a lot of space storing numbers. The way I interpret this with the leading zeros in "RE-00512," is very specific confirmation that I'm only being shown a small taste of what's available, and it only happened after I started to downplay the earlier events.

As such, I'm now more concerned about getting the full treatment from the phenomenon than I am about coming off like I'm crazy or putting on airs, so I'm not going to equivocate or otherwise demand proof. I'll just flat-out tell you that this is my strange tale of the paranormal and the Men in Black.

The Stripper and the Men in Blue by "Emily"
– As told to Steve Ray

"Emily" grew up in rural East Texas, in a part of the country where most houses have had a Sasquatch sighting, part of a family who traced their lineage back to French nobility and, legend has it, to faerie nobility.

Emily credits her faerie blood for her beauty and her occasional precognitive dreams (usually when life was bad), and she did have at least one childhood encounter with a strange light and missing time.

Bored with small-town life and her self-converted Mormon relatives, she moved to Dallas at age 15 and became an exotic dancer before she was old enough to drink.

Barely 5 feet tall and 100 pounds, dark-haired and busty, Emily was doing very well for herself, both dancing in the clubs and as arm candy for rich, old men.

"I like it best when they're too old to even try to get in your pants, but they'll pay you $2,000 a week just so they can act like they have a hot girlfriend."

In 2013, Emily was dancing at Spearmint Rhino, and during day shifts there, she would play cards and flirt with patrons at the Pokertainment funny-money Hold-Em table.

Right around the summer solstice, Emily dreamt that: "People from the FBI" in dark suits approached her at work. One of Emily's regulars was with her at the card table, and the FBI agents sat down and said they knew who she was and wanted the power she had, and they wanted her "to help them with the stargate," whatever that was.

Then the FBI agent took out a densely worded contract and threatened to ruin the lives of her favorite customers, her dancer friends, and even a sick child Emily was fond of, so she got scared and signed it without reading.

A couple days later, Emily dreamt that the day-shift bartender was being impersonated by an FBI agent, who gave her "clumsy emotional tests" and made her watch a crowd of strippers on the main stage dance together wearing two-foot-high Japanese wood-block shoes.

The agent kept asking, "What have you learned?"

The following Wednesday, as she drove in to work, Emily saw a cat run across the road, then back, then out again, where it sat on the median and stared as she drove by. Not only had the cat moved unnaturally fast, far faster than any normal cat could run, but she recognized it as a rare hybrid that costs $5,000 per kitten, a detail only a girl with expensive tastes would notice.

Later that night, Emily was hanging out with a customer on his birthday. They ruled out going to Denny's (free breakfast be damned) and instead they were celebrating at the Fare Room, a nearby BYOB strip club.

The two were sitting and talking at a small table near a thirty-foot-high dance cage. It was by no means secluded, but in a club like that, people try not to interrupt what might be an intimate conversation.

So it was very weird when a man walked right up and started talking to Emily. He was tall, with blond curly hair, wearing blue jeans, a blue shirt, and brown dress shoes, and he said, "You two look like the only normal people here. Can I sit and talk with you?"

Understandably, Emily's friend sent the intruder off with a curt, "No, go away." The man left the club, then came back in and talked with one waitress while looking over at the disturbed couple, not ordering mixers, but just asking questions.

Emily didn't recognize the man in blue as any of the pimps or drug dealers who try to work the area, and he left for good after twenty minutes, a short stay for having just paid a $20 cover charge. His behavior was so strange that Emily wondered if he was trying to keep tabs on her for the FBI, "just not wearing a suit."

After she went home, Emily was kept awake all night by cars driving by every twenty or thirty minutes, despite living on a cul-de-sac with no through traffic, and she saw a figure in black looking in through her ground-floor window.

Two days later, Friday afternoon at 3:30, it was Emily's turn at work to start her dance rotation. From the stage, she could see a man sitting oddly at the card table, wearing a blue polo shirt, blue jeans, brown shoes, with short blond hair. He had a drink but was waving away all the dancers who approached him.

This man in blue came up to the stage during Emily's song, but did so while she was already dancing for another customer. He threw a $5 bill at her, but -- unlike a normal club customer -- did not stay for her to come over, say thank you, or otherwise demonstrate her appreciation.

Instead, the gentleman went back to sit at the card table, where he did not play, but ordered one more drink and kept checking his watch and staring at her. As soon as she was done with her stages, Emily approached the customer, who said he had to go, stood up, and walked out. He had stayed at the club roughly twenty minutes.

Two weeks later, after allowing a self-appointed mentor to take her to an Oklahoma casino, Emily headed to her favorite Thai restaurant. Nearby construction made the eatery almost unreachable, and since she was his only customer, the owner could chat with her about this and that.

During the conversation, an older man with brown hair in an untucked blue plaid shirt and blue jeans came in and asked Emily, "Do you mind if I talk with you?"

He had the same personality as the man in blue at the Fare Room, but since her evening was free, Emily saw a chance to learn what these suspected "FBI agents" were up to.

This new man introduced himself as "Paul" and – after a little small talk -- invited Emily to join him for a drink.

She probed him, asking "You look familiar. Do I know you from Rhino?"

Paul said he hadn't been to that club. He also didn't like any of the places Emily thought they could drink, and suggested The Magic Time Machine, a restaurant where the staff dresses like celebrities past and present. She drove her car, and Paul arrived separately in his recent-model black Cadillac Escalade.

Paul did not seem like a normal person. He used three very forgettable pick-up lines on her, looking very nervous, but "not like a pervert, more like someone worried they are failing their objective."

Their waitress was dressed like a Barbie Doll, and Paul not only reacted to her in character, but encouraged Emily to join in, saying "it's more fun when you role-play." Emily declined, saying that she preferred mind-fucks.

Emily ordered a martini, shaken not stirred, followed by a vodka and Red Bull, while Paul babysat a lone gin and tonic and made weird conversation with her, saying he could tell she was going to be famous or a celebrity.

Born on December 8th, Paul was a Sagittarius, and when Emily described her sign, Pisces, as "either good or bad," he wanted to know what it took to bring out her bad side. Did Paul know that she had more dreams of the future when she was feeling negative?

When the Barbie-Doll waitress asked who Emily would be if she could be anyone, Emily said Elizabeth Taylor. Paul thought that was interesting,

"You remind me of my assistant Elizabeth. Are you half Asian? Your mannerisms remind me of her."

Emily said no, she was a model and actress and had just quit dancing, but Paul thought he may have seen her at Spearmint Rhino before and asked for her dance name.

Emily made him guess for it, which went as follows:

Emily: "I'll give you three guesses."
Paul: "Does it start with a vowel?"
Emily: "Yes."
(Whereupon, Paul guessed a lot of A names.)
Emily: "It is not an A."
Paul: "Does it start with E?"

Emily: "Yes."

Paul: "Elle?" (the name of Emily's younger sister)

Emily: "No."

Paul: "Emily?" (her actual dance name)

Emily kept answering Paul's questions with questions, just to see what he would do, revealing that he lives in San Francisco and works with computers, though he was vague when asked for details -like he didn't want to trip up his own story. He said he travels all over the world for his job and thought maybe he had seen her in L.A.

The Barbie-Doll waitress now asked Paul what character he'd most like to play, and he said a psychologist or therapist, joking that "she's in therapy now," but not giving an actual name.

Emily had had her drinks and was ready to go. Paul awkwardly invited her home with him, not like a nerd is awkward, but like he had no experience acting human. She said no, but gave him her phone number so she could observe him again.

One final note: On the off chance Paul's people might still be watching her, when Emily left The Magic Time Machine, she made two U-turns and took a roundabout way back home, but as she was about to get on the main road, someone pulled directly in front of her, in a white Ford pickup truck with two alien-head stickers on the back.

27.

"He had a narrow, sunken face"

Neville Jacques is a social worker who lives with his wife, Barbara, in Cleveland in the North East of England. He has a casual interest in UFOs and the paranormal, while Barbara is generally skeptical of such things. Neville shares with us a strange, MIB-themed encounter he and Barbara had in Fuerteventura, Costa Caleta, in 2012...

I listened to your show on *Coast to Coast* about Men in Black recently. The header photo for that gave me some relief! Let me explain: I was on holiday with my wife in Fuerteventura, Costa Caleta, in the Canaries, November-December 2012. We were walking back to our hotel on a very long promenade walk. It was close to 4 p.m. There were other people milling about. It's kind of high up on a volcanic rock face, directly at the sea's edge and a wide open area. We noticed about 100 meters in front of us a tall thin man, at least 6 foot 2, with a big rimmed black hat, round feature hugging black sixties type sunglasses, a long sleeved shirt and a light colored jumper (sweaters to you Yanks) over his shoulders and long trousers!

What made it more strange was his face looked white as if it was plastered in sun block, (whiter than white). We both laughed and watched him walk towards us. I got the feeling he was watching me, although I couldn't see his eyes. As he drew closer it became apparent that it wasn't sun block: It was his skin! He had big hands and long fingers, also very white, kind of in front of him, not by his sides!

When we where about 5 feet from him, I noticed his skin was almost translucent. That's the only way I can describe it! His sunglasses covered all of his eye area and wrapped around the full socket area and were round and black. He had a narrow, sunken face, had a very angular jaw and prominent cheekbones. He looked to be in his sixties or so. I am a social worker for older people so the age would be a good guess.

When he was passing us, he turned his head looking at me and spoke, with a kind of acknowledging manner, and said something that I and my wife couldn't understand or describe as human language. It was high and low pitched all at the same time and very short, that's the best way to describe it! Strangely we didn't look back to see where he went or take a photo, both of us don't know why we didn't and I got the feeling he was watching me from me first noticing him.

We got back to the hotel and I could not stop thinking and talking about the encounter with my wife, I kept telling her he wasn't from here, his clothes weren't right. In fact, he was totally alien in appearance to anyone I have ever seen in my life. I went to bed that night and didn't sleep much, every time I tried to go to sleep all I could see was him and I thought about the encounter for the rest of the holiday.

I searched the internet for all types of albinos that I could find for months after but couldn't find a match for him. Then I found your interview on Coast to Coast and bingo! The artist's impression of the Man in Black was him, only without the hat and glasses.

It still freaks me out to this day Nick, we can still not explain it!

28.

"They looked odd
and retro"

The child of a practicing occultist and a natural medium, Felix grew up in an atmosphere that encouraged metaphysical study and introspection. After a variety of jobs in the family's hometown of Blackpool, England, at the age of 28. S/he moved to Manchester to attend University as a mature student in 1982, reading for a degree in Theology and Religious Studies, which was awarded with Upper Second Class Honors.

After graduation, Felix volunteered as an adult literacy tutor and taught in Manchester University's Extra-Mural Department, creating its first academic course in Tarot. S/he later gained the Postgraduate Certificate in Education (submitting a thesis on Haitian Voodoo - also a first.)

During the latter part of the 1980's, Felix became chronically ill with fibromyalgia and had to cut short plans for a career in education. However, life brought other opportunities including activism for equal opportunities as both a disabled person and as one called to live between the genders. S/he has a particular interest in the intersection of spirituality and gender as a cultural phenomenon and is training as a Skilled Helper.

Felix shares life with his/her fiancée in Old Trafford. S/he also spends time invigilating exams, messing about in a boat and catering to the whims of assorted cats...

First of all, I'll set this account in context. I'm a transgender person - born female, living as androgyne and a natural psychic. My father was a practicing occultist; he was a member of the Golden Dawn in the '50's and a lifelong student of magic and metaphysics. My mother attended a spiritualist church and had a number of experiences that assured her that the death of the physical body was not the end of the personality. I would describe myself as an eclectic occultist and researcher.

I was brought up to accept there will always be phenomena that we may not understand and to be critical but not dismissive of anything odd that happened to me. I was born in 1954 and raised in Blackpool, from where I moved to Manchester in 1982 as a mature student, reading Theology and Comparative Religion.

In 1981, I lived in an attic bedsit in one of the big, old houses that had been converted into flats. It was just one room, really, with a Baby Belling cooker in a former wardrobe and a sink in the corner, providing hot water through a Creda. My bed was in a corner with the window behind me and to the right. The door was past the foot of the bed on the left hand wall.

In December 1980, I had had a pregnancy terminated; this had been a stressful time, physically and mentally but I was coping OK. I wasn't working but had worked as a bar supervisor and had lined up a job for the summer season so I was taking it easy for a while.

Now, in spite of my interest in matters mysterious, UFOs and alien contact have never particularly grabbed my attention. I'd read a little about claims of alien abduction but had no books on the topic and of course there was no internet back then.

Very late one night in, I think, February 1981, I woke suddenly to see the semi-transparent form of a youth in 1930's type clothing, writing at the table under the window. He seemed unaware of me and I just thought, "That's nice; he seems happy enough. I wonder if he's a spirit or a memory imprint on the house?" turned over and went back to sleep.

I don't know how long after this I was woken by the sound and "feel" of visitors. I sat up in bed and saw two men in the room, absolutely solid and "real", assumed they were police and wondered how the hell they had got in.

I recall saying, "What?" and they approached the bed. I lay down, grabbing the quilt in fright but they were absolutely impassive and did not address me directly. One took a gadget a bit like a mobile phone in appearance and "scanned" me with it. He told his companion – I'm not sure whether I heard this with my ears or telepathically - that this was a female 20-30 years and was infertile due to contraception (or a term meaning the same). I had recently started using the Pill.

The other man took a stroll around the room, examining its contents. He seemed very amused by anything that plugged into the wall - the Creda heater and my radio-cassette (the latter is especially important) - and commented, smiling, "I can't believe they're still harnessing it from an external source." I felt that he was familiar with people generating their own electricity via their bodies.

All the time this was going on, I couldn't move or speak; it was as if they held me in a trance or catatonic state.

The next thing I knew it was morning and I was alone. I reached down, shaken, to switch the radio on and was surprised to hear just a load of static. On inspection I saw it had been tuned to an area where there is NO station. Now, I always had it tuned to Radio 1 (a lot of young folk did then) and never touched it. It was the last thing I recall the man picking up.

It wasn't until later that evening that I put together the pieces of the visit and thought, "Men in Black!"

In appearance they were very similar and dressed identically, like twins. Both were around 5'8 – 5'9 in height with a slim build. Their complexion was a bit olive/jaundiced. I'm not sure about their eyes and what hair I could see was black. They wore beige, straight cut raincoats over dark trousers and shoes with white shirts and black ties and each had a beigey-brown fedora. They looked odd and retro and had an aura, not of menace, but of indifference to humans; I felt they looked at us as specimens in a laboratory.

I have never told anyone but my parents this story and

always had the feeling I was not meant to discuss it, at least for a number of years. As decades have passed, I thought I would share it with you. I hope you found it interesting!

Again, many thanks for your excellent book on this topic – I'm presently torn between the tulpa and the time-traveler models but I'd rather they didn't come back to tell me. ;-)

Felix was not done with the Men in Black, however. There is the following too:

My mother tells me that when she was a young girl in Blackpool, living near the airport at Squires Gate, she had an experience that shook her to the core.

Aged around 13 or 14 years - so that would be pre-war 1936 or so - she was coming home from work as an apprentice dressmaker one winter evening around 6pm. To reach her house, she had to walk along Squires Gate Lane which is a long road that goes past the airport and had fencing all around made of wooden panels. She was on the opposite side to the airport preparing to cross when a light caught her eye, seeming to shine out from behind the fence as a paling was moved to one side. It dazzled her a bit and she was puzzled as security was tight there and she'd never seen anyone or anything messing with the fence.

While she was thinking this she was astonished, and then terribly frightened, to see a "little man" emerge, followed by two others, both holding lamps or electric torches and moving quietly so as not to disturb anyone. Now, by "little" she says they were probably around her own height, making them around 5ft nothing as she was a tiny woman.

They were slender but a bit stocky around the middle (padded clothing?) and had spindly arms and legs. Their attire was an all-in-one kind of black or dark-coloured jumpsuit with a hood. Their faces looked very pale, almost luminous, peeping out. She remembers their eyes very vividly - BIG and bright with black pupils. They reminded her of pixies from children's books but she "knew" they were "something else".

There was absolute silence, no traffic and she was freezing cold, from fright as much as the winter weather. Suddenly, one of them caught her eye and "looked almost as startled as I was". To her horror, he - she felt they were male - began to take steps to cross the road, indubitably to "make contact" with her. She was too terrified to scream so she ran, silently, a slightly longer route home, never stopping for breath until she reached the front door where her pounding alerted my grandfather.

All she could say was that there were, "Men in Black" (I kid you not) at the airport field and was helped in, half fainting. Of course, granddad assumed she'd been assaulted and dashed out to inspect the road where he saw nothing amiss. When at last able to speak coherently, she described the beings to my grandparents who mused she may have seen the Boggarts - Lancashire imps - having an evening out!

My mother says she "knew" that the little men 'knew' she

was "a child" and told each other this by a kind of whispering language which wasn't English but which she nevertheless understood, perhaps telepathically. Even in her eighties, she could recall this experience with utter clarity as one of the strangest and most terrifying of her life, worse than any during the War.

The daft thing is, I always went with the "Boggart" theory until a couple of months ago when, reading something on UFOs the MIB/Greys connection went "ping". Of course, the "Quatermass" stories conflated demons of antiquity with 20th Century alien visitors and I should have at least picked up on this by watching the films!

We often sat in that field together, me and Mum, and I never felt it was an evil place - just "odd" somehow, even when the buttercups and daisies were in bloom and the fence had long since been demolished.

29.

"His staring eyes are lit up with a disturbing glare"

Steve Ash is a London based Fortean Writer and Researcher who has had a lifelong interest in UFOlogy. He is currently working on his latest book *Mind Wars, UFOlogy Reconsidered.*

The Men-in-Black, A Personal Perspective
– By Stephen J. Ash

It was a bright morning sometime in the mid 1970s, probably around 8:30am, most likely late Spring or perhaps early Autumn. I was 13 and making my way to school. I'd been fascinated with the UFO phenomenon since my earlier childhood, after witnessing a couple of illuminated discs fly silently over my garden, in a precise synchronised trajectory.

But I think the topic was still firmly in the entertainment zone for me then. After all aliens that close - as I then conceived them - was a bit too scary a thought not to be dismissed as some ingenious advertising hoax. I knew little of aeronautics then. But it awoke a possibility for me, and I had soon devoured books by Jacques Vallee, Brad Steiger and John

Keel, as well as further developing a love of science fiction. Therefore I was fully cognizant of the mythology before a perspective-changing event that was about to occur would nudge me into a new direction.

A week earlier, I had embarked with a friend on a school project, a mandatory requirement that term. The topic of my choice was unsurprisingly "The Flying Saucer Mystery". My year master was supportive and suggested we visit the South East London headquarters of BUFORA, which we had found in a local telephone directory.

We enthusiastically agreed, not least as it was a wonderful chance to bunk off school for the afternoon. The walk wasn't far, and after a short stop off at the local fish and chip shop we arrived at our destination. This turned out to be a suburban flat with no obvious sign of cutting edge UFOlogical activity. We rang the doorbell and waited. But there was no reply. We rang again. A curtain twitched but no one answered the door. Disappointed, we returned, to the fish and chip shop.

It's a week later and I'm now contemplating this project as I walk down a long straight back street with only a few slight bends, giving a clear view off into the distance in both directions. It is strangely quiet, and I was the only traveler in the street, but then the road was not as busy as it is today, and it was early morning, so only in hindsight would this seem significant.

In this distance, I spy a man walking towards me. He's a long way off, a mere black silhouette. He gets closer, I note he is actually dressed entirely in black. My predictable speculation on this is at first a humorous one. I stop chuckling to myself as he gets closer, and I see a black suited figure in a pork pie hat, walking stiffly towards me. Slightly uneasy, I rationalize that lots of people dress that way, and besides he's not wearing wraparound dark glasses. He gets very close and in my increasing apprehension I note the suit and hat are ill fitting and the man is very pale, almost zombie like, and walks with a mechanical gait.

We are about to pass in the empty street as I further notice his weird appearance, a gaunt, emaciated figure, with bulbous eyes, his black suit and black shirt crumpled, his black tie pulled into a tight knot, his too-small pork pie hat perched on a pale bald head. I resolve to stare ahead myself and ignore him as we pass.

As we do, I feel an irresistible urge to look at him. I turn my head, he gives me a huge insane grin, which seems to reveal a wired up mouth. His staring eyes are lit up with a disturbing glare. The look will be etched into my memory forever. At that stage I think I was aware of the grinning man and the corresponding reports of similar MIB. I quicken my pass as he moves past me and behind, wanting to put as much distance as I can before turning to have another look. When I do a minute or so later the road is completely empty, there is not a trace of him or anyone else. I stop and wait a few moments and look down the street, scanning doorways, observing parked cars, listening carefully. Nothing.

As I completed my journey I tried to rationalize the experience. Surely he was just a nut, he saw my alarm and capitalized on it. But where did he go and why did he look like what John Keel called "the Cadaver", one of the rarer manifestations of the MIB? Perhaps he hid in the bushes or dodged into a doorway or a parked car, yet I heard no doors open or close, and it was so quiet, certainly no car engine had started.

He'd also walked a long way towards me, so what were the chances his destination was just beyond the point where we passed? Slim to none, I think. We were quite near an alley, but I am certain I had not reached it by the time we passed, though I had by the time I turned around, could he have doubled back? But all this seemed to indicate he was actively hiding, a disturbing thought in itself. I brushed the experience from my mind, but it constantly returned to haunt me.

Since then, I have analyzed the memory to exhaustion. Have I elaborated on it over time as is so common with old memories, added elements from my reading, and partly fabricated it in reflection? I don't think so; the experience was so disturbing, it was instantly embedded into my memory and I'm sure it happened pretty much as I remember it.

Perhaps he was simply the hiding loon I had tried to dismiss him as, the world is full of strange people. I subsequently learned, many supposed MIB were just eccentrics or worse. But why encounter him a week after the visit to BUFORA? I'm a great believer in the "Cosmic Joker", that apparent influence behind random events and coincidences, that seems to be having a laugh at our expense. But this seemed a little too much.

Perhaps the visit was no coincidence? It"s also likely that many MIB are hoaxers, often linked to UFO groups. But this happened near my home several miles from the scene of the visit, so how could they trace me? No one had followed us when we left the BUFORA address. Sure we had school uniforms, our school was identifiable, but I doubt very much that the school would have given our addresses to enquirers, even before pedophile awareness!

Unless they were officials. I briefly toyed with the theory the MIB were an elaborate stunt pulled off by Intelligence Agencies. Was BUFORA under surveillance, even infiltrated? But the idea that such an organization would then invest its time and resources in scaring a 13 year old on his way to school exposed the absurdity of the idea. All that was left was coincidence.

Yet there was something strange about the man, an aura, not of malice, however. I never felt threatened;, it was a feeling of some dark humor. The stranger wanted to scare me and was enjoying it very much. Strangely it is this apparent dark humor, not dissimilar to my own, that today leaves me with almost a sense of affection, or at least of respectful awe. Even if it was a hoax or spontaneous prank it was a brilliant one. But there was also something unworldly about him. Though perhaps now I am elaborating. He was certainly strange, his wired up mouth looked like he had the worst dental brace in history, or perhaps three of them, and he was clearly not in the best of health. Years later I saw a picture of Conrad Viedt from *The Man Who Laughs*, also the inspiration for the Joker in *Batman*. The expression was identical.

But what I also find interesting about this experience is that it marks the first time I took the whole UFOlogical phenomena seriously. If, as is commonly thought, the MIB are silencers with an agenda to scare people away from the subject, he had an entirely opposite effect. But then so do the more obvious silencers for many people.

There is a strange duplicity in the phenomena. Following this, I became briefly obsessed with the UFO phenomenon as a teenager, an obsession that would lead to a fascination first with weird science and later with the occult. But perhaps most influentially with philosophy, a turn also encouraged by my subsequent reading of science fiction. This would lead to my eventual achievement of a Master's degree in the Philosophy of Science at a top university, something that I wonder would have been different had I not had this experience, my family being solidly working class, with few if any ever attending university. Perhaps I attribute too much to these events, or perhaps not enough.

This wasn't the last time I encountered the MIB, perhaps. Over two decades later, long after my UFO enthusiasm had waned in adulthood, and I had taken up more esoteric interests, I found myself called back to the subject by my classmate Clive, the very person with whom I had started that school project. He too had been affected by the experience, which had eventually led him to spiritualism long after I had lost contact with him. When we met again, he was still enthused with UFOs and wanted me to join an ambitious psychic circle to contact the intelligences behind the phenomena, which he still believed were extraterrestrial, a hypothesis I had abandoned long before.

This is a story in itself which I shall recount as part a forthcoming book but shall pass over for now. What is relevant is the attention this endeavour attracted. It was widely advertised in the usual magazines, so it should not have surprised us that it attracted odd phone calls from eccentrics and other interested parties. Clive maintains he was contacted at a bus stop by a man claiming to work for the M.O.D who seemed unusually interested in him. Perhaps a coincidence. Less dismissible was the black car that slowly drove past his front door as we stood outside, and took our photograph with a flash, in broad daylight, before speeding off! Perhaps the source of this was different to my earlier experience, but like it, it fitted an established pattern of MIB behaviour and reignited curiosity in the whole subject.

Another possible encounter was indirect and almost comical. I had been involved with an esoteric group, with zero relation to the UFO phenomena, about ten years after my experiences in Clive's psychic circle. We met in a friend's flat on the top floor of a council estate in a backstreet in East London. One evening there was a knock on the door, and our host answered it. I don't remember if we heard the conversation, it was a small flat, or if it was relayed to us by the host, but the essence of it was that a couple of foreign sounding men were asking for a person with the same first name as one of our five friends present (apparently no surname was given.) The friend in question rejected this saying it couldn't be him as he had told no one of his presence there that night, and so our host returned to the front door to inform them they had the wrong address.

Meanwhile we discussed the strangeness of the event. Who visits a council flat, one of dozens in the block, on the top floor of an obscure council estate in the back of beyond, and asks for someone by their first name alone? At the time I jokingly commented something like 'it could be worse they might have been all dressed in black!' But on the return of the host, he informed us that actually they were! This would become doubly strange when it was found that they did not seem to have visited any of the neighboring flats as far as could be ascertained! The guest in question decided not to return to that group afterwards.

A final anecdote occurred around the same time. A friend of mine of long standing, whom I knew to have claimed psychic abilities, on hearing my school days experience surprised me with the announcement that they were actually trained to locate an individual by remote viewing anywhere in the world from a photographic or even a drawing of the person. I was naturally curious and produced a sketch of the individual, to the best of my limited artistic ability, as well as supplementing a clear description. My friend focused on this, then suddenly broke off quite alarmed. They had located the "individual", but it was quite unlike anything they had ever experienced, and in fact quite disturbing, almost animalistic. They were clearly unnerved by the experience and refused to try again.

All of these accounts are isolated events of course and should be treated as such, as they may have quite different ordinary explanations. But taken together they seem to me to form a pattern, whether a real one it is hard to say of course, but it is a pattern in perfect correlation with established MIB lore. This has brought me to the conclusion that there really is something very odd going on here and that the MIB phenomena cannot be easily dismissed as something prosaic or unreal.

So what do I think now after nearly twenty-five years of studying and investigating the MIB phenomena on and off? Well, my full conclusions will be presented in a chapter of my forthcoming book exploring the whole UFO mystery, but I will briefly state it here as it currently stands. The simple answer is extreme puzzlement.

To begin with, a critical investigation of the available evidence is not very encouraging for anything but a sceptical opinion. I'm fairly convinced that the "MIB" who visited Harold Dahl and others in the late 1940s were nothing more than government agents in typical dress code of the period. Likewise the handful of more impressive encounters with MIB reported by members of the IFSB in the early 1950s seem to be often attributable to an eccentric occultist and former security guard called Gordon Deller, who typically favored black attire and had pretensions of deep knowledge of UFOs, which he would only cautiously reveal to the chosen few.

The rest seem to be rather tenuous impressions in an atmosphere of paranoia. Which really only leaves Albert Bender's astonishing account, and the paranoia it generated, which unfortunately varies over time, between something which sounds like more government agents snooping around to something distinctly supernatural, on different tellings.

Furthermore: Gray Barker's role in the creation of whole 'mythos' is decidedly suspicious, particularly given his predilection for hoaxing. It is in fact very easy to dismiss the entire phenomenon of the 40s and 50s as misidentification and hoax.

The 60s however are slightly different; some genuinely strange encounters are recorded, but even here the whole phenomenon is conditioned by and rooted in the dubious foundations of the 1950s. While at least one famous MIB of this period, Tiny, now appears to have been identified as a man with severe mental and physical health issues and an obsession with UFOs and vampires (although he does appear to have been working with other people who stayed in the shadows.) All this is not helped by the lack of a serious scientific study and the sensational hack writing associated with it.

On the other hand, some of the accounts, particularly those from John Keel, do seem a lot harder to account for, even given Keel's alleged "investigative gullibility" and "'journalistic elaborations". There are sometimes hints of a well-funded intelligence operation, but to what purpose remains a mystery. Yet other accounts, assuming they actually happened as told, seem distinctly paranormal. The only thing that seems clear is they are not from outer space!

On the strength of the known evidence alone, I think I would be tempted to dismiss the whole thing as nonsense, if it was not for my own experiences, which put me in a strange cognitive space between personal empirical evidence and a negative rational analysis. Assuming my intuitions about my own experiences are true, then I can only say the phenomenon is very subtle and very well hidden, something pretty impressive in itself.

John Keel's classification of the MIB is particular interesting given my experience with something very like "the Cadaver". Unfortunately I have never experienced anything remotely like the Oriental MIB, who he argued were the most common of the "mystery men" (that is if we dismiss the more Caucasian types as cranks and hoaxers, or even agents of some incredibly secret government agency, which Keel didn't entirely), but given one apparently correct hit I am inclined to respect the other!

There is a serious problem with such categories and classification however. The classic MIB is in fact a generalization of many individual cases, with some similarities but also many differences between them. Both mythos exposed witnesses and investigators alike and tend to focus on the similarities and ignore the differences. This tends to generate idealized descriptions which real encounters rarely accord with completely. Even Keel's more specific categories and differentiations, though well researched, are not accompanied by his presentation of a list of identical encounters: They are an approximation taken from a limited number of partial descriptions, and possibly Keel's own experiences.

But perhaps we can't really expect more given the subjective nature of human perception and the vagaries of witness testimony even in established crimes. Given my experiences, I'm inclined to take Keel's account at face value. Though I think his attempts to show the MIB have been present for centuries are somewhat subjective and less impressive.

There are a number of leads to follow in MIB research, but they tend to lead off into strange tangents. One of the strangest was from source John Keel kept anonymous, who claimed the MIB were from the "Nation of the Third Eye", and their symbols were the "eye in the triangle" and the "lightning flash", a claim that has never been repeated as far as I know. The latter symbol recalls the Neo-Nazi rants that have been uttered by one or two supposed MIB (the fake Tiny was fond of praising Hitler too, so perhaps this goes with the pathology.)

At the opposite end of the scale, several mystery men encounters in rural areas have been associated with gypsies or indigenous peoples who imply they have some secret occult association, something not beyond the bounds of possibility given the interest some native shamans express in UFOs.

On the other hand Keel claimed the vampires of the Balkans as closely related to his MIB. Others, including myself, have sometimes wondered if the MIB are actually time travelers, given their timeless sartorial style and their brand new vintage cars, or even something like the Agents from *The Matrix*. But all these leads fail to go very far and most seem to be dead ends. One thing that does seem clear however is that the MIB are not simply interested in UFOs; they are interested in all paranormal phenomena. In fact, quite often they seem to be part of that phenomena. But we don't really have enough data to draw any definitive conclusions from all this.

My own preliminary conclusion is that the MIB phenomena as a whole is a myth based on a range of diverse causes, from which an urban folklore and paranoid fantasy has been generated. However, within that myth I think there is a very real and mysterious phenomenon, that is either paranormal or based on some technology beyond our current knowledge, whether human or non-human. But what is most surprising about this is that the core phenomena seems to be either consciously hiding within the smokescreen of this broader myth (perhaps even assisting its formation), or is an intelligent phenomenon actually shaped by that myth. I think as with the UFO phenomena in general this gives it a very important place in any scientific investigation of reality and our position in the Cosmos.

30.

"I remembered thinking: I don't think they had pores in their skin"

In her very own words...

During the late 1970s, a Galactic Scribe named Lavandar was enlisted to act as witness/guardian/recorder of many diverse ET projects, some of which have concluded, while some are ongoing.

An author of two channeled books, "Quartz Crystals: A Celestial Point of View" and "50 Questions and Answers," Lavandar was assigned to guide many celebrities and politicians with regard to their missions. As a human born fully conscious of her identity and mission, she was directed to witness or lead projects for the next thirty years and record galactic information as it was transmitted and/or witnessed.

However, the chronicles of the projects and knowledge imparted was to be held and protected, at all costs, in a bank vault until a signal was sent to release the codes for Starseeds, Walk-Ins, Light Workers and Indigos.

This vital information has been locked in a one-way vault since 1983; chronicles and transmissions could be added, but not released or removed, until the codes were sent to open the vault. Lavandar is a Galactic Shaman using Galactic Astrology to identify star marking codes in an astrological chart.

Her discovery of Star Markings continues to activate those with starseed codes into further DNA Galactic Activations showing "natural state" and "rites of passage." For further information, see Lavandar's website: www.starseed-hotline.com

I've had a lifetime of "high strangeness" and I was taken out into the desert by George Van Tassel and he told me some very profound things, in 1977; the things I would be involved in, in the coming years. What he told me was very shocking as he told me about walk-ins, ET implants and advanced technologies that were 3,500 years ahead of our consciousness on the planet. Some of these technologies we know about now, others are too "out there" to even be explained by our conscious minds. But, in 1977, that was very shocking news.

One of the things George Van Tassel told me that day that we walked out into the desert in sight of Giant Rock was that I was going to be an ET experiment and that I would have to walk through experiences that some would call "The Twilight Zone." And he would download things to me that were so mind-blowing and then he'd stop and he'd wait to see how much more he could tell me before he would start to speak again. We walked and talked for about 3 hours.

I can still see him pointing to Giant Rock and saying, "One day, when that rock cracks, it's gonna activate you to release your 'light information.'" So 22 years later on Feb. 21, 2000 it mysteriously cracked.

When the rock cracked, I was taking care of my ill parents. I pulled out my mother's paintings for her to sign and there was one she hadn't finished and it was a picture of sand dunes.

I said: "Oh, I think I'll finish this for you, mother."

She said: "Well, you can't paint."

I said: "I'll paint it with George and I."

She looks at me and she goes: "And when are you going to release that story?" That was the day, at that moment and time, when Giant Rock cracked.

It was shortly after that that I got a phone call telling me of Giant Rock being cracked, either by lightning or some other force. I remember thinking as I was hanging up the phone, "Finally, I can release the information from the bank vault as I see clearing that the ET's got this whole thing timed." (*Crack Between The Worlds* is listed in the archives of the Starseed Radio Academy Shows on www.blogstalkradio. com/starseed-radio-academy).

In 1979, I was living in Sarasota, Florida and in August of that year – I think in the first week of August - I started having some severe pains. My mother had just arrived the day before. She called the ambulance and they took me to the hospital and they said: "You're passing a kidney stone." They took x-rays of it. I guess it really shocked them because I guess it wasn't. It was metallic; it wasn't a calcium deposit.

The doctor said: "Are you allergic to anything?"

I said: "You can't give me sodium pentothal because I'm a UFO contactee and I was told to never allow it in my body. It would probably kill me because of my genetics." He just raised his eyebrow. He disregarded my request. I was in the operating room and they were getting ready to take this object out – which was not calcium but metal. They gave me a shot of sodium pentothal and I died.

They went and got the paddles to bring me back and hit me one time, which cracked my sternum.

A booming voice came in with a big blue light – a big, round, indigo-looking light just floated down in the middle of the room and a voice said: "Don't touch her again."

The doctors and nurses fled the room. That energy, whatever was there, brought me back. The way I found out about that portion of the story is that my hairdresser's sister was the lead nurse in the room, and she told her sister what had happened to me. But they all had to sign a piece of paper saying it never happened and noone's to ever talk about it. When they came back in, there I was, alive. First, they were discussing what to do, because it was just so bizarre. So, I was wheeled to recovery and apparently, I'd been talking.

I don't know what I said, but when I woke up there were three Men in Black standing at the foot of my bed. They started asking me questions that I cannot remember. I know that I answered them. I remember when they were standing there I didn't feel fearful. They looked like they were about 5'

5"; they were about of equal height and their skin was a little lighter than the normal. At first I thought they were triplets. Their shirts were shiny; an oyster-shimmer. Their hair was exactly alike. It was dark and slick, like they put grease on it.

I remembered thinking: I don't think they had pores in their skin. And another thing: they were standing there and I reached over to get a glass of water and when I looked back they were gone. They hadn't had time to walk out of the room. As soon as they left, I remembered thinking: I probably shouldn't have said that.

So, when my doctor came, he was very strange and he started asking me questions and again I had drugs in me, so I just told the truth. And he gave me two prescriptions and told me I could go home. Well, my mother and I, we got into a fierce argument. She didn't like all this UFO talk at that time and told me that if I didn't shut up they were going to lock me up.

So, we got home and she decided she couldn't be there anymore and said: "Well, just call your friend. I'm going to the airport; I'm leaving." So she left.

She wrote down the two prescriptions they had given me. It was funny because they called in the pharmacy to get those prescriptions filled and then they handed me the prescriptions, which I got to have it in writing what this was, even after this happened. So, my mother gets home and she calls me. I think I took two doses of whatever they gave me.

She calls me and she says: "I looked in my medical book

and when these two things are taken together they make a person go insane. Please stop taking them." And so, I did; I stopped taking them.

I was left with a portion of my brain was opened and out there. It was like it opened up something in me, where I couldn't function like a normal person. It was after that I really started experiencing a lot of other things. Within about a month, I was hit by lightning – on a bridge in Sarasota. That, of course, opened up another channel into my brain.

In 1980, I bought an A-frame house in Cripple Creek, Colorado. I didn't know it then but it was on the land where Nikola Tesla caught lightning in a jar.

All these Tesla kids starting showing up, knocking on my door saying: "Can I walk on your property?"

I'd say: "And why?"

They would say: "Well, Tesla caught lightning in a jar behind your house."

And I said: "Well, who's Tesla?" The minute I said who's Tesla I had these rushes through my body. By the way, there was a huge gold vein under my house; later it became a portal. A lot of ETs came and went through this portal. It was from here that I would write and secrete away "light information" that wasn't to come out for many years. A curious thing about these Tesla Kids' appearance: they all started looking alike, dark hair, dark eyebrows and most of them resembled David Copperfield.

After awhile after several of them starting talking to

me about the same subjects I thought: *The Boys from Brazil.*
What's going on here? This is in 1980 and for the next 7 years
I got to know a lot of them, and when a couple of them were
killed because of their "free energy devices," I felt it was time
to disconnect.

Finally, one day, I said: "I quit; I'm not doing anymore
work in this area." I jumped on an airplane and I went to the
Caribbean, to the island of Aruba where I lived for 9 years.
One day I took my chair and umbrella way out on the far end
of the island and I thought: I'm just gonna erase that part of
my life. It's not working.

Here comes this young kid walking up to me and he says:
"I was contacted by a spaceship that told me that if I came to
Aruba, and if I walked out here, on this particular day, at this
particular time, there would be someone that would talk to me
about Nikola Tesla."

I just about flipped. I thought: I can't get away from these
Tesla Kids. But it all started – when I track back – it had
something to do with what happened to me in the operating
room in Sarasota, Florida; which in turn took me back to 1977
when George Van Tassel told me that I would experience "out
of this world events" that I was to journal and keep locked in
a bank vault for 25 years.

It has now been 37 years and I have released some of this
"light information" on our Starseed Radio Academy Show.
Crack Between The Worlds is now a project being considered
for a film and mini-series. It will show the comings and

goings of ET's on the planet and how through the blood-lines, many ET experiments have been conducted through many centuries, including during the times of Atlantis, which seems to be the moment in time when most of the experiments were put in place for the evolutionary state of the people and planet Earth.

31.

"Nothing entities like Men in Black say or do should be trusted"

Christopher Loring Knowles is the author of the Eagle Award-winning *Our Gods Wear Spandex: The Secret History of Comic Book Heroes* (2007, Red Wheel/Weiser), co-author of *The Complete X-Files: Behind the Series, the Myths, and the Movies* (2008, Insight Editions) and the author of *The Secret History of Rock 'n' Roll* (2010, Viva Editions). You can find several books' worth of his pop culture and weirdness work at http://secretsun.blogspot.com I'm very pleased to present for you a new paper from Chris on his views on the Men in Black...

MIB-UFO: Virtual Reality and Reality Tunnels
– By Christopher Loring Knowles

I'm one of those handful of weirdos who believe flying saucers are real physical objects guided by intelligence but do not believe they are filled with spacemen from another planet. I believe both of these things for the very same reason- too many people have been witnessing these things for too long for a truly reasonable individual to dismiss them all as illusions. But the fact that so many people have seen so many UFOs for such an incredibly long time effectively rules out extraterrestrial vehicles, at least to me.

I love *Star Trek* more than anyone but the distances between stars are huger than we can imagine. And even if an advanced civilization has mastered the warp drive,) I truly doubt they'd come here and behave anything like flying saucers have since prehistory.

UFOs are a cyclical phenomenon and we're in a typical fallow period at the moment. UFOlogy itself is plagued by a "kill your darlings" fad: mainly elderly nuts-n-bolts types who resent that the saucermen didn't whisk them off to Zeta Reticuli as back payment for their years of tireless advocacy. Now they spend their time attempting to debunk cases they once clutched dearly to their bosoms, alienating their onetime allies and arousing nothing but smirks of contempt from the real skeptics.

But the actual debunkers are an even sadder lot, seen as irrelevant dinosaurs - or worse- by the angry young nihilists steering the skeptic movement towards atheist activism and politically correct witch-hunting.

The conspiranoid set doesn't have much interest in the topic, other than to throw around talismanic buzzwords like "Project Blue Beam" (an old internet hoax that may have been concocted by elements connected to the Collins Elite) and "HAARP" (a real project that is used as a rhetorical fallback for any number of phenomena it has absolutely nothing to do with) at it.

The UFOs don't much care; sightings and encounters continue under the radar and sooner or later they'll burst back into the public consciousness. And given the defeated, deflated nature of what passes for our modern civilization, there's a good chance the next flap or wave could trigger a gusher of fear and loathing in the body politic.

It's hard to justify these fear projections, even following the liberal rules of evidence in UFOlogy. Only the most extreme- or gullible- UFO researchers can argue that the phenomenon has caused physical damage to human beings- certainly nothing even remotely approaching mass murder, oppression and slavery that human beings inflict on each other every day of the year.

A skeptic would argue this is because the UFO phenomenon only exists in the human imagination. And perhaps they'd be half right.

Just as I can't find any compelling evidence that UFOs are interplanetary vehicles, neither can I find compelling proof of modern physical contact with physical "aliens" as we would commonly understand such a thing. The fact that there's been such a variety of creatures reported in these accounts argues against the literal, physical reality of these experiences.

But there is compelling evidence that something else is going on and has been for a very, very long time. Most people familiar with UFOlogy know that Men in Black showed up before, if not in a different context, particularly in America. You have a long tradition of encounters told in the most sober of fashions, with beings good, bad and indifferent as angels, demons, fairy folk, and on and on and on. Occult UFOLogist Allen Greenfield points to the three angels who appeared to Abraham in the run-up to the destruction of Sodom (Genesis 18:2) as an early appearance of MIB-like entities.

There is an ancient key that can unlock this puzzle. "Abductees" and "Contactees" have often described their encounters as terrifying, but I've yet to see any compelling evidence of real physical harm. But these contacts do remind me of ancient encounters that were enshrined into the Mystery religions of the ancient Mediterranean, so much so that "terror" prepares their minds for contact with divine beings and became common practice in many cults.

Even a cursory read of the ancient Mithraic Liturgy of the Paris Codex -- which tells of an abduction via a beam of light through the air into a metallic flying disk filled with strange beings (and doors and instrument panels,) who take the initiate on a tour of the heavens -- shows that these encounters long predate the science fiction trappings of extraterrestrial contact that dominates the conversation today. This is no small thing: this liturgy belonged to the most powerful cult of its day, a warrior religion that commanded the rulers of the known world and whose writings were instrumental in Carl Jung's conception of the Collective Unconscious. There are of course other explanations for this phenomena - night terrors, sleep paralysis and so on-- but even without those cases you still have an interesting corpus of contact including a whole host of daylight encounters. You may be familiar with the many parallels between fairy lore (fairy being a catch-all phrase here for any number of supernatural but non-divine beings) and modern abduction accounts-- the focus on sexuality and reproduction, the hybrids.

Skeptics might use these parallels to dismiss it all, but I see it as confirmation that contact is taking place in a constructed environment that behaves a lot like our modern conceptions of Virtual Reality. How appropriate that the gods of the ancient Mysteries insinuated themselves into our modern conception of Virtual Reality from the start: witness the Loa and Orisha manifesting themselves in Cyberspace in the work of SF novelist and VR theorist William Gibson. Or note that the most popular VR narrative of all time, *The Matrix*, also features blatant MIBs as the heavies (as does its 1998 prototype, *Dark City*). Both films are absolutely drenched in Mystery symbolism as well.

I see this all as a return to first principles.

There are greater mysteries though, ones which the Men in Black phenomenon raise. Our concept of physical reality is a reductive construct, created to facilitate a consensus that allows the day-to-day responsibilities of life to be seen to. No small thing, that. There are conscientious objectors to this construct though, albeit ones you can't lynch or toss in prison.

Throughout history we've seen accounts of beings and objects that appear and disappear at will, often in front of large groups of ordinary citizens, sometimes in front of cameras. They don't care whether or not anyone believes in them or can explain them. They do what they want and don't worry much about the consequences.

The UFO isn't easy to explain away, though not for lack of trying. But these anomalous beings are a different story. I've encountered a couple of them myself, and the lingering question in my mind is still "what the fuck was that?" But the fact that other people across huge expanses of time and geography have had identical experiences leads me to believe it was not my imagination.

One thing people who have these experiences can speak to is how random, and *irrelevant* these encounters can be, at least at first. They seem to explain nothing, they accomplish nothing, and they confirm or deny no deep-seated need; they just are. Dreams can usually be traced to psychological urges, hallucinations less so but still seem to fit into some larger psychic context. Encounters with what UFO heretics call "Ultraterrestrials" usually make no damn sense at all. Or appear to, at least.

And then there are Men in Black. There are a whole host of explanations that can easily explain the phenomenon as government agents, pranksters, or simple hoaxes. But what matters is not the encounter so much as the result. What was the result of this encounter? If it radically changed the course of a person's life, chances are pretty good that something important is at work. If they scare people, they just as often as not scare them into a heightened awareness of deeper realities than the shampoo commercial reality the snitches and debunkers and schoolmarms want us all to live in.

I'd go even farther- I think we'd sooner trust the reality of a demonic encounter than an angelic one. We tend -- and with good reason -- to dismiss stories of angelic encounters, whether in their Biblical or Space Brother incarnations. In fact, a lot of people are inclined to interpret angels as devils in disguise; leading their victims to disaster by seducing them with pretty promises. It's why so many people distrust the New Age movement, with its syrupy love and light bromides. In contrast, a Man in Black seems to be a what you see is what you get proposition.

If you really take the time to see past the skeptic-believer dichotomy, the UFO phenomenon takes on the feeling of theatre- a high theatre in the skies. The high weirdness of the entire UFO drama, the juicy bits that the fading nuts-n-bolts crowd dismisses out of hand, starts to feel less anomalous than typical the more you really look at it. If you dispense with the pulp sci-fi trappings and set your sights before 1947 on the timeline, what seems bizarre and ridiculous starts to make a lot more sense.

Many of the old UFO legends -- the men like Kenneth Arnold and Aime Michel, not to mention John Keel and Jacques Vallee -- dispensed with the invader from Zeta

Reticuli mythology and came to realize that UFOs and their aftershocks have been our intimate companions since we lived in trees and caves. But this exegesis is a lot less comforting than the idea of space saviors to the believer, and heart-stoppingly terrifying to the Debunker.

We all have a normality bias. In fact, for nearly 25 years I dismissed what I now see as a classic UFO encounter as a "swamp gas" sighting with some weird after-effects. And for good reason; I happened to be driving through the Great Swamp of New Jersey at the time. But it wasn't until I actually *researched* swamp gas (or foxfire or Will o' the Wisp or faerie fyre or take your pick) that I realized there's no way it could have been methane ignitions.

I was my own debunker: I latched onto some weak but convenient excuse. It didn't hold up to serious scrutiny but I set it all in stone anyway. I realize today I did so because the experience was pretty unsettling, and not unlike any number of Man in Black encounters. And it wasn't until over a year after I first submitted this essay to Nick that the pieces began to fall into place.

It happened one night (sometime in early autumn 1988) when my wife, myself and our infant son were driving Long Hill Road (known to the locals as Great Swamp Road) to the 24-hour Pathmark supermarket. We kept weird hours at the time. We had a Volkswagen Rabbit convertible, and since it was warm, we probably would have had the top down.

At some point, I noticed three stars in formation over the

tree line; a bit on the bright side, similar to Venus on a good night, but nothing out of the ordinary. They weren't blinking so they probably weren't planes or choppers and it would be years before anyone around here heard of Chinese lanterns. I wouldn't realize until much, much later that many classic UFO cases began the exact same way.

The trees were in full bloom and blocked out the sky on much of the drive, but every time we came to a break in the treeline I noticed the positions of the stars changed. And *noticeably* so, from a straight line to a triangle to an inverse triangle and so on. We're talking distances of a hundred feet or so, so our vantage point didn't justify the weird change.

The wife and I were very interested in astronomy at the time - our bedroom had a giant, glow-in-the-dark star map in front of our bed and I had gotten a telescope for my birthday, which I was playing around with in the back yard. So I was very interested and familiar with stars (I have a globe with the major constellations just to my left as I write this.) I wasn't thinking about UFOs at the time, so I don't remember exactly what I thought it was. Just weird.

It got weirder.

After shopping, we were getting ready to leave and a strange man approached us in the nearly deserted parking lot, very much intruding into our personal space. On the face of it, he was no Man in Black. Actually, he looked more like a typical CSI cop debunker-type; big and bloated, late middle-aged, balding, bespectacled and unkempt. He spoken in a Eastern

European accent, feeding my wife some bullshit story that he had some baby furniture he was trying to get rid of.

The entire conversation seemed extremely strange. I seem to remember he wanted us to follow him to his house to pick it up - it was getting close to midnight. And my wife would later remind me he also offered his services as a sitter.

As I loaded the groceries I spotted a slovenly older woman watching all of this, apparently his wife. She was leaning on a beat-up old (70s vintage) Ford LTD wagon, her arms stiffly folded at her chest looking like a woman watching a nightmare she didn't have the will to stop. I wasn't having any of it. I physically placed myself between the man and my own wife and dismissed him with clenched-teeth pleasantries. I'm six foot five and was pretty fit at the time, so the guy backed off and returned to the car. As we were getting ready to leave I noticed him sitting in his darkened car, smoking and staring at us very intently. His wife's face still looked etched with a mix of anger, fear and humiliation, even in the dark.

To some abduction researchers this might sound like a typical screen memory of an encounter- a young family driving down a dark, deserted country road, strange lights in the sky, an anomalous encounter with a creepy stranger speaking in a foreign accent. In some ways the image of the couple's faces in the car reminds me of stories you might read of abductees seeing their captors' faces illuminated by instrument panels. And to be honest, in my retellings of this story over the years I could never picture us actually shopping beforehand.

To Debunkers, always eager to excuse or rationalize any kind of predatory behavior directed at young children, I'm making something of nothing. A Debunker would also double down on the setting of the sighting and insist that it just *had* to have been swamp gas.

On the face of it, there really is not much to this story. Weird stars in the sky (which could have been anything) and a creepy encounter with a potential sexual predator that was defused through physical intimidation. However, what really interests me here is the synchronicity and symbol that accompanies so many encounters with UFOs. And the more I thought about it the stranger and more resonant it seemed.

Nuts-n-Bolts theorists have no time for the bizarre after-effects of UFO reports because they still believe that they are just one case from UFOlogy being accepted as a legitimate science. But if I knew next to nothing about the high weirdness aspect of UFOs and MIBs at the time of this sighting, my research since made me realize just how strange this event (that was barely a footnote in my life) really was.

As I like to caution people who ask, lights in the sky are just lights in the sky. In my opinion, it's not until you do the math - the UFOlogical Kabbalah - that you can begin to determine the true weirdness of a sighting or experience. I don't always agree with John Keel or Jacques Vallee, but it was Synchronicity that forced me to take the UFO topic seriously again after many years of ignoring it and it was Synchronicity that allowed me to understand it in an entirely new way.

First, the setting. The sighting took place in the very same swamp mentioned in Orson Welles' notorious *War of the Worlds* radio broadcast. Again, the setting was the reason this event was my "swamp gas" story for a quarter century.

Second, the sighting took place right around the corner from The Raptor Trust, a refuge for birds of prey. At the time of this writing, their website features two magnificent white owls staring back at you. This sighting took place while Whitley Streiber's *Communion* was all the rage in UFO circles. That book brought the theme of "owls as screen memories" into the UFOlogical lexicon.

When I was a kid, my mother was an obsessive collector of owl figurines and prints. Shortly before I was born (Spring/Summer 1966) she had a recurring nightmare while she napped on the couch that a "witch" was coming into the house to kidnap her. I later learned that there was a huge UFO flap in the area at the time.

Third, a week after I originally submitted this essay to Nick, David Bowie released the video for his single *The Stars (Are Out Tonight)* from his album, *The Next Day*. The video begins with Bowie and Tilda Swinton playing a married couple who are being stalked by two bizarre figures inside a food market, and menaced by them outside the store. One looks like a classic MIB, the other like a supermodel. They are also driving a classic (70s vintage) MIB black sedan. *That* synchronicity certainly caught my attention.

Though most critics interpret *The Stars* to be about

celebrities, the lyrics (mostly) and video (clearly) demonstrate it's another manifestation of Bowie's alien/occult/UFO obsession. One of the songs feature on the deluxe edition of *The Next Day* is *Born on a UFO*, a parody of Bruce Springsteen's *Born in the USA*.

And there is the fact that my wife's name -- Elizabeth Knowles -- is etymologically identical to Elizabeth "Betty" Hill, who had her own world-changing encounter with the hidden world one balmy evening. Facts I was unaware of at the time, I might add. This is no small thing - my son was a year old at the time that this very strange man showed such a great interest in he and my wife.

Why is this significant?

Because the Barney and Betty Hill drama -- the most notorious abduction in UFO history -- *all began on my wife's first birthday*. And that too began with a couple on a lonely road looking up in the sky and seeing a star that didn't look quite right. That realization took the wind out of me.

Ever since I realized that my swamp gas story was no such thing, I've been puzzling over the strange conjunction of the sighting and this very strange encounter with this creepy and enigmatic stranger. I knew the two were somehow related, I just didn't know how. And in my imagination, he seemed like a tulpa, creating an itch I couldn't scratch until I could make that connection. Now I realized the purpose of that encounter; it was so I wouldn't dismiss that sighting as a trick of the light. I surely would have forgotten the sighting otherwise.

It also made me think about those Men in Black. For years people have puzzled over their motivation, threatening UFO witnesses, sometimes even before the witnesses ever told anyone else what they'd seen. They carry on strange conversations, dress and behave strangely. I would argue they do so *in order to be remembered*, so that witnesses and experiencers don't dismiss or forget their experiencers. Have the Men in Black ever actually silenced anyone? Did they really intend to?

I don't think so. The Men in Black naturally connect in my mind to the Mothman incident. That's another one of those cases that skeptics love to nibble away at, but you really can't argue with the Silver Bridge collapse. I do agree with Vallee that there seems to be something intentionally irrational and maddening about these kinds of phenomena. But at one point I realized I had a number of strange connections to the Mothman drama, culminating in the fact that the editor who "discovered" me was herself from Point Pleasant and remembered the Silver Bridge disaster.

What infuriates the rationalists about these phenomena is that ultimately they realize that these things are taunting them, mocking their pretensions to godhood. Tranhumanism is science's latest attempt at apotheosis, but it's fascinating to see rationalists so deeply divided over it.

In fact, many scientists are deeply divided over quantum physics as well. The more advanced science gets, the more esoteric it becomes and the contentious it becomes within the ranks of science itself.

Are UFOs some form of science that is so advanced it no longer is recognizable as a science? It's as good an explanation as any. It's why the endless attempts of the talking heads of *Ancient Aliens* to reduce godhood to 50s era Sci-FI can be so frustrating for this writer. I think if these ancient astronauts did indeed exist, their science is still inexplicable to us, so much as to be magic. Certain factions within the corridors of power would prefer you believe that the entire UFO phenomenon was all just some Cold War psyop. But to do so you have to somehow pretend that the Robertson Panel, Project Grudge, the Condon Report, the Roswell Report and the countless armies of well-paid government media debunkers are all magically negated by Strawberry Ice Cream Man.

If it was a psyop, it seems there were a hell of a lot of agencies who weren't in on the gag, not to mention all of the universities, media outlets, scientific laboratories and all the rest of the entire establishment who did nothing but rather violently deny the existence of UFOs for 70 years or so.

Come to think of it, I actually *do* believe it was a Cold War psyop, just not one cooked up by anyone down here. Its purpose was to keep the shaved apes from blowing each other up. But then, I've always believed that the UFO phenomenon behaves exactly like a spy or surveillance program, being a fan of spy thrillers myself. And seeing how it looks a lot lately as if we're headed for Cold War II, I'm thinking that the UFOs and MIBs will be out there again too, making sure that this new Cold War doesn't get too hot.

Final Words

On the morning of July 16, 2015, I opened the Word file of the book you have just finished reading. It was my intention to complete the final edit of the manuscript before it went to publication. At the very moment of opening the document, something unexpected happened. I heard a loud noise come from one of the rooms in my apartment. Puzzled, I left my office and had a look around.

The maintenance people at the complex in which I live had been working all morning on the outside portion of one of my exterior walls. And, the vibration of their hammering and tools had shaken a framed picture off my interior side of the same wall and it had fallen to the ground, shattering the glass all across the carpet.

It just happened to be a framed, old letter written by Albert Bender, the man who pretty much kicked off the whole Men in Black controversy in the early 1950s. Not only that, I have at least fifteen framed images on the walls of that room. Of all the ones that could have shattered, it was an MIB-themed one.

Now, I know it was the vibration of the maintenance tools that caused it to fall off and shatter, but the coinciden-tal timing of (a) me opening the Word document, (b) the specifically MIB-themed picture falling to the ground, and (c) the glass breaking at the exact same time was, at the very least, "interesting."

Coincidence? Based on everything that has come before my "Final Words," I seriously doubt it. A warning from the dark-suited ones? Maybe...

About Nick Redfern

Nick Redfern works full time as a writer, lecturer, and journalist. He writes about a wide range of unsolved mysteries, including Bigfoot, UFOs, the Loch Ness Monster, alien encounters, and government conspiracies.

His previous books include *The Zombie Book*; *For Nobody's Eyes Only*; *Secret History*; *Monster Files*; *The World's Weirdest Places*; *The Pyramids and the Pentagon*; and *Chupacabra Road Trip*.

He writes for the *MUFON UFO Journal* and *Mysterious Universe*. Nick has appeared on numerous television shows, including Fox News; The History Channel's *Ancient Aliens*, *Monster Quest*, and *UFO Hunters*; VH1's *Legend Hunters*; National Geographic Channel's *The Truth about UFOs* and *Paranatural*; BBC's *Out of this World*; MSNBC's *Countdown*; and SyFy Channel's *Proof Positive*. He can be contacted at:

http://nickredfernfortean.blogspot.com

Acknowledgments

I would like to offer my very sincere thanks to everyone who contributed to this book; without your fine material it would not exist. I would also like to thank my tireless literary agent, Lisa Hagan, and my editor and publisher, Beth Wareham, for their excellent work in bringing the book to fruition.

35237086R00145

Printed in Great Britain
by Amazon